KU-023-892

# THE BEACH BOYS' PET SOUNDS: THE GREATEST ALBUM OF THE TWENTIETH CENTURY

by

## Kingsley Abbott

Helter Skelter Publishing

# CONTENTS

# CONTENTS

# FOREWORD

When I was fifteen years old and a high school student in Laverne Oklahoma I worked for a neighbouring farmer ploughing fields out on the flats where the wind really did come sweeping down the plain. I drove a tractor that pulled a 'twenty foot one-way,' a monstrous contraption, across a vista of limitless horizons and took lunch in the extreme luxury of a 1956 two-tone, two door Olds ninety-eight coupe that my father had quite illegally given me for my birthday. One day, while sitting there munching on a peanut butter and jelly sandwich and surveying the oceanlike panorama of rolling wheat stubble before me while idling my engine and running the air conditioner, (Yes, the Oldsmobile was some piece of work!), I heard a song on the automatic/footswitch/signal-seeking radio that altered my perception of reality. It was called "Surf City."

The reader must realise that I had no idea whatsoever what 'surf' was – I had only vaguely heard of The Beach Boys and certainly no idea that the Jan and Dean hit had been penned by a kid close to my age named Brian Wilson. (The phrase 'two girls for every boy' came through like gangbusters however.) I was determined to find out what 'surf' was and shortly thereafter – in a serendipitous twist of fate – I was to learn. My father, a Baptist minister, fulfilled a lifelong dream and moved our burgeoning family to Colton, California, the burial place of Wyatt Earp, a quiet community nestled close to San Bernardino – 'Berdoo' in surfer parlance, the 'Inland Empire' in Chamber of Commerce Speak. How is a poor boy from Oklahoma to explain the heady, almost narcotic effect of suddenly being thrust from the lonely furrowed wastes of Northwest Oklahoma into the balmy, night-blooming jasmine-scented, pheromone-wafting midsummer twilights of suburban Colton? I have a vivid sonic memory of my first night there, after the moving van had departed, lying on my bed amid the chaos of my as-yet unstowed gear and hearing the song "In My Room" by The Beach Boys – theirs seemed a funny name then because I had never seen an ocean – emanating from what must have been more than one household at the same time. It was out of sync and overlapping, yet warm, right and reassuring in the dark. To my most sincere recollection, that is the first time I ever heard them.

I am listening to *Pet Sounds* again as I write this and wondering as always about the mysterious mental terrain traversed by Brian Wilson during the previous years that culminated in the creation of this most glorious work of art. We have interacted and our paths have crossed from time to time in the years since. Glen Campbell, who recorded so many of my songs, was a fellow artist of Brian's at Capitol and equally frustrated by that regime's short-sighted view of profit in the foreground and artistic achievement and lasting worth on the far horizon. Most will know that Glen toured with the group and for a time sang Brian's parts and that he inherited a track from them and overdubbed and released it. A decade had passed when Brian came to my thirtieth birthday party and approached me to present a bottle of champagne. He took a close look at me. 'You have dark wings around you,' he said sympathetically. Truer words were never spoken. We worked together, albeit at a distance, on "Adios" with Linda Ronstadt (on the album *Cry Like A Rainstorm, Howl Like The Wind*) and he stunned me yet again with his flawless singing and instinctive, perfectly correct vocal arrangement. He honoured me when he insisted that I write the orchestration for Tim Schmidt's version of "Caroline No" on the *Stars and Stripes* LP, the last time, unfortunately, that I ever saw Carl. I sit here again marvelling at "God Only Knows," illuminated admirably by Kingsley's painstaking unravelling of the facts and figures and fictions behind the creation of an album that so inspired the Beatles that *Sgt. Pepper* was 'an attempt to equal *Pet Sounds*.'

They were words that Sir George Martin spoke to me personally with his familiar knowing smile and the corners of his eyes crinkling with subdued humour. But after all is said and done miracles are only miracles because at the end of the day they are unfathomable. The most memorable and striking among them occur only once. The Beatles never got back together and we have been waiting a long while for their successors. The well-meaning wife of a program director at a radio station once asked me during an all-too brief moment of glory, 'When are you going to write another "By The Time I Get To Phoenix"?' If I had answered I would have said: 'that would be impossible, but if it *were* possible, what would be the point?' Brian Wilson no doubt has many great musical triumphs ahead of him and I hope to have the good fortune to be there and witness, if not share in, some of them. Will there ever be a sequel or an equal to *Pet Sounds* discovered in some dark and dusty attic on a reel of discarded two-track analog? Perhaps we should not want there to be. *Pet Sounds*, like a magical fairy tale or an impossible love story, could and did only happen once … upon a time.

Jimmy L. Webb
Mar 16 2001 Nyack, New York

# AUTHOR'S INTRODUCTION

For me, it all dates from May 1966 when, as a tentative Tru-gel teen, I managed to get put through to the suite at the Waldorf where Bruce Johnston was holding court and extolling the virtues of *Pet Sounds* to anyone who would lend an ear. I listened enthralled as I spoke for the first time to a real live Beach Boy who actually sang over the phone to me! He told me all the news of the current recording and said he would arrange to get a copy sent to me and, true to his word a couple of weeks later, I received a U.S. copy of the album straight from The Beach Boys' publicist Derek Taylor. I had been a total Beach Boys convert since hearing "Surfin' Safari," and had bought everything by the band that I could lay my hands on. Now was a chance to get the full blast of a whole new album before its U.K. release. The Dansette was opened, and the rainbow labelled disc placed carefully on the turntable for the first time, and I began to listen…

Then, suddenly, an almost immediate feeling of letdown and disappointment crept over me. What? No summer beach lyrics… no chuggin' surf rhythms… no counterpoint surf harmonies? But wait, there's "Sloop John B!" I loved that one with all those wonderful vocals, but these other tracks…what are they all about? Fortunately, undaunted by my initial misgivings, I spent the next few days re-listening frequently to *Pet Sounds*, and gradually something began to change. It was impossible to define at first, but as the joy of "Wouldn't It Be Nice" and the romanticism of "God Only Knows", with its inter-twining tag vocals, began to seep in, a subtle and melodious flower slowly blossomed before my ears. A livelong love had begun.

Continual exposure to *Pet Sounds* over 35 years has not dimmed that love; rather it has deepened and increased it. It mattered not that, as we subsequently discovered, The Beach Boys aside from Brian were only responsible for the vocals. It mattered not that the U.S. market had deemed the album a comparative failure (partly because it was thumpingly successful in Britain). What mattered was that here was an album that could bear, indeed positively thrive on, continued re-visiting and reveal more nuances and hidden aural treats over the passing years.

For a very long time now I have known how special an album *Pet Sounds* was, even without the musician's language and knowledge required to properly explain why. It has often been called a "symphonic" album by critics who never fully explained the term. Did they mean that it was as good as a classical piece? Were people likening it to the work of a composer like Bach or Beethoven, and if so it which ways? I simply did not know. All I knew was that it was very, very special, and in my wide appreciation of rock and pop albums during their life span (almost exactly fitting my own) I could not find anything that came close to it.

The idea for this book arose out of a comparatively casual conversation in London's Helter Skelter bookshop about how wonderful it was that Brian Wilson had begun to tour *Pet Sounds* in its entirety. It set us wondering why books had been published about other "classic" albums of the sixties, seventies and eighties, while a dedicated book was yet to appear about the long player that consistently topped – or at the very least appeared in the higher reaches of – all the Best Album polls run by the music press and the wider media. There and then we decided to rectify the situation. My premise was a simple one: to write a book about the best pop album of the twentieth century.

Whilst I have sketched an outline of certain aspects of The Beach Boys' history within the coming chapters, it was never my intention to retread the group's chequered career other than where it had a direct bearing on the *Pet Sounds* album. Those who want to know more about the band's history are directed to David Leaf's excellent biography *The Beach Boys and The California Myth* and other works namechecked in the bibliography.

Initially I had planned to incorporate into my narrative a series of "Interludes" written by a selection of musicians of varying age and background that bear testament to the personal and musical effect of the album. However, my requests prompted a greater response than I ever dreamt possible, and consequently, I was forced to extract shorter pieces from these wonderful contributions for presentation within the main body of the text. I hope that all the writers will understand and forgive me.

The book could not have happened without the help of a great number of people. Interviewees have included Brian Wilson, Bruce Johnston, Tony Asher, David Marks, Hal Blaine, Carol Kaye, Don Randi, Billy Strange, Michael Melvoin, Paul Tanner, Kim Fowley, Jeff Foskett, Darian Sahanaja, Timothy White, Andy Paley, Rodney Bingenheimer, Rick Henn, Mark Linett, Harvey Kubernik, Daniel Rutherford, Marilyn Wilson and David Kessel. I thank them all for the generous amounts of time they have given me. Valuable discussions and insights have come from three good British friends, Chris White, Charlie Brennan and Andrew Doe, who have both helped to give me a wider and deeper perspective. Robert Mattau's wonderful photos and designs have enriched the later stages of the book. Thoughts, help and contacts have come from Alan Boyd, Patrick

Humphries, Philip (PF) Sloan, Joe Foster, Frank Laehnemann, Stefan Kassel, Carrie Marks, David Leaf, Carol Kaye (especially Carol!), Jean Sievers, Michael Brunsmann, Tommy Steele and Janet Grey at Capitol Records HQ, Jo Pratt and Sam Locke at EMI/Capitol British offices, Elliot Kendall, David Bash, Brian Battles, Duglas Stewart, Dave Mirich, John Porteous, Bob Stanley and Sean O'Hagen. Special thanks go to Stephen J. Kalinich for his poem that ends the book.

The wealth of written testaments sent to me have proved to me how much genuine affection that there is for Brian and *Pet Sounds*. For their inputs, my thanks go to John Carter, Sean Macreavy, Andrew Loog Oldham, Tony Rivers, Sid Griffin, Robin Wills, Chris White, Nancy Sinatra, Jennifer Baron, Jeff Baron, Margo Guryan, Dave Frishberg, Louis Philippe, Todd Fletcher, Eric Matthews, Brian Kassan, Scott Brookman, Gary Pig Gold, Jeff Larson, Sean O'Hagen, Luke Abbott, Peter Lacey, David Scott, Sandy Salisbury, Duglas Stewart, Harvey Kubernik, Neal Umphred, Hal Blaine, Brandt Huseman, Johnny Navin, Marc Carroll, Linus of Hollywood, Philip Sloan, and Andrew Gold.

Special thanks and great affection go to all the lovely people at Helter Skelter: Sean Body, Mike O'Connell, Tracy Bellaries and Caroline Walker. Thanks also to all the people who have assisted in many other direct and indirect ways: Martin and Chris Lawford, Micky Groome, Stuart Talbot, John Francis, Bryan Thomas, Freeman Carmack, Caroline Ross, Susie & Neil at Poptones, Wes & Hazel Kent, Big Al Brett, Chris Allen, Peter Thomas, Watson Mac, Marty Wombacher, James Crowther, Barry at Long Wave Instruments, Pat Gilbert, Andrew Male & Keith Cameron at *Mojo*, Mark Paytress & Lois Wilson, Michael White, David Bash, Koki Emura, Miranda Filbee, Val Johnson-Howe and the members of Beach Boys Britain, Mike Grant and the members of Beach Boys Stomp, Stephen J. McParland, Peter Doggett, John Reed, Andy Davis, Tim Jones, Joel McIver, Daryl Easlea and all at *Record Collector*, All the 'Spectropoppers', Lynn Ziegler and the members of the "Warmth Of The Sun" site, Elaine Abbott, The Franks family, Rosie Abbott, Luke Abbott, Ian Drakard and Molly Crampton. Very special thanks must go to Jimmy Webb for the foreword. He came on board most enthusiastically through the good offices of his talented sons (Christian, Justin and James plus Rick and Neal), currently touring as The Webb Brothers.

Mostly though, thanks go to everyone who was involved with the making of the album that forms the content of this book: the company employees, the friends and relatives, the engineers, lyricist Tony Asher, the musicians, The Beach Boys... and of course the man who provided the conception and realisation of the whole wonderful project... Brian Wilson.

# BRIAN WILSON ON *PET SOUNDS*.

Brian had enjoyed an early afternoon vocal and instrumental rehearsal at home with four of the band members in early March, after which he took time to talk especially for this book. It was at a time when it looked likely that the tour would visit England. He was happy, relaxed and positive, and very interested in the whole idea that a book was being written purely about the album. After chatting about more specific points and clarifications about the album's development, I asked him for some overall reflections:

"When *Pet Sounds* came out, I didn't know how well it was received in Britain at first. I knew that some people like Paul McCartney said how they really liked it. He thought it was very special. I kinda think it's a great little album too! My favourite song is definitely "Caroline No," but do you know what I am most proud of on that album is the melodies. People often ask me about how satisfied I am with it, but when I look back I certainly wouldn't want to change anything; it was only done once!

Recently we started touring with the band and it was going really well, and we made that *Roxy* album, my wife and my managers said that we should try and do a *Pet Sounds* tour. Well, they had to really prove it to me, as I didn't think it could really be done. We worked real hard to get it perfect, really perfect, and we've shown that we can do it. I'm really enjoying all the singing. On the tour we have had a different orchestra in each city, and they give us warm, rich feels. All the orchestras are pretty good, you know! Now we hope that we're going to bring the tour to Europe, and I'm really looking forward to that. Maybe soon we'll be doing some new recording with my band before we come, and some of that may include Andy Paley. I'd never consider doing a fully instrumental album you know; I'd always have to have vocals. I always want vocals!

I'm really honoured that there will be a book just about the *Pet Sounds* album. Gee, that's great! Will you have the book ready when we come to England? I sure hope so. I'll sign a copy for you, and I want one too! I'll look out for it!"

– Brian Wilson, March 2001

## *PET SOUNDS*: TRACK LISTING

Wouldn't It Be Nice (Wilson/Asher/Love)
You Still Believe In Me (Wilson/Asher)
That's Not Me (Wilson/Asher)
Don't Talk (Put Your Head On My Shoulder) (Wilson/Asher)
I'm Waiting For The Day (Wilson/Love)
Let's Go Away For Awhile (Wilson)
Sloop John B (Traditional: Arr. Wilson)
God Only Knows (Wilson/Asher)
I Know There's An Answer (Wilson/Sachen/Love)
Here Today (Wilson/Asher)
I Just Wasn't Made For These Times (Wilson/Asher)
Pet Sounds (Wilson)
Caroline, No (Wilson/Asher)

# Chapter 1
## HOME, FAMILY AND FRIENDS.

*"Hawthorne, that's a crummy town. It was not like Bel Air, Beverly Hills. I lived at 3701 West 119th Street; it was a small house."*

– Brian Wilson

*"My dad was an asshole, he treated us like shit and his punishments were sick. But you played a tune for him and he was a marshmallow."*

– Brian Wilson

In contrast to Europe, stoically enduring prolonged post-war rationing and struggling to regenerate both materially and mentally, America in the 1940s and 1950s was a land of growth and plenty. The sprawling area of Los Angeles in particular enjoyed a period of unprecedented expansion, with a huge building programme establishing suburbs where there had only been scrub. It was in one such suburb that the children that were to form America's most successful music group grew up.

Murry and Audree Wilson moved to the new suburb of Hawthorne in 1945, bringing with them their three-year-old son Brian Douglas and new baby Dennis. After living frugally elsewhere in L.A., they managed to scrape together a $2,500 deposit for a two bedroom bungalow at 3701 West 119th Street, on the corner of Kornblum Avenue. Hawthorne was some twelve miles South-East of Central L.A. but despite the development program, it was initially a fairly barren estate, devoid of trees and far from the Californian paradise depicted by *National Geographic* or Hollywood. Nevertheless, to Murry and Audree it represented a step further toward attaining their dream.

By the time he moved to Hawthorne, Murry Wilson had a variety of sales jobs behind him, and he was on his way towards attaining one of his personal goals – that of running his own tool and lathe company, which he would do in the fifties. Meanwhile, his family continued to grow with the birth of Carl in December 1946.

American family structures of the fifties and sixties were rigidly hierarchical. Parents commanded respect from their children, who addressed them as "Sir" and "Ma'am". Despite his own difficult upbringing from a violent, hard-drinking father, Murry was an extremely strict disciplinarian. Though he loved his sons, Murry was prepared to use physical punishment and other tactics of intimidation to assert his will. He was also a firm believer in traditional masculine values, and expected his sons to follow suit. Accordingly, the Wilson family's yard was always full of bicycles and sports equipment. The boys' world of Tootsie Rolls, baseball gloves, white socks and Coca Cola epitomised white American male youth of the time. Murry put great store by success in sport, and he hoped that his eldest boy Brian would do justice on the playing fields to reflect his growing physical stature. Once Brian had left York Elementary School for the much bigger Hawthorne High, which had over 2000 pupils, Murry began pressuring Brian to succeed in baseball, football and track. Brian had some talent, but he lacked confidence and the pressure of his father's great expectations only exacerbated his self-doubt.

Counter-balancing Murry's zeal for the typically masculine pursuits of work and sport was another passion that can be traced back to his own difficult childhood. Murry's parents, Bud and Edith, owned a fondly-treasured piano, and Murry and his sister Emily's harsh upbringing saw family music sessions relieve the bouts of drunkenness and domestic violence. When they later set up homes of their own, both siblings ensured that music was an integral part of family life. Murry and wife Audree would regularly gather their sons around the piano for group singing, as would Emily and her husband Milton Love with their family.

The Loves had a home on the corner of Mt. Vernon and Fairway in the Baldwin Hills district. They were more prosperous than The Wilsons, running a sheet metal business that thrived on the back of the local development boom. In the mid-fifties, Emily and Milton's extended family would converge on their house for Christmas musical gatherings, where a selection of family members – including both Brian Wilson and his slightly older cousin Mike Love – would perform individual turns. Mike Love was the eldest of three brothers and two sisters, and naturally found personal as well as musical connections with the elder Wilson boy.

Murry Wilson's musical interest was not confined to family sing-alongs; he was an enthusiastic amateur composer who had begun writing songs with specific artists of the day in mind. Murry was desperate to bolster his self-esteem by succeeding in this competitive arena. In fact, when one of his songs, "Two Step, Side Step", was featured live on the radio on the Laurence Welk Show, it proved almost too much for him. Brian recalled in his autobiography, *Wouldn't It Be Nice*, that his father "couldn't suppress the emotion. It was strange to see this bear of a man reduced to blubber... he left the room… too embarrassed to cry in front of his family."

Brian considered his occasional sporting success a mixed blessing, but he was quick and enthusiastic to respond to the musical influences around him. This was all the more surprising considering that Brian was virtually deaf in his right ear. Despite this handicap, Brian displayed a precocious natural ability. Indeed, his parents date his ability to hum melodies back to the age of two. As a young teen, Brian's natural shyness would diminish in musical situations at school and church, where he happily and unashamedly excelled singing solo and with the choir. Murry and Audree organised junior accordion lessons for him, but despite Brian's progress, helped by his uncanny aptitude to play by ear, they couldn't afford to continue. Nevertheless, Brian began to take all available opportunities to teach himself on the family piano. This quickly became an escape from family conflicts and the pressures of school, where he only achieved fair to middling results in academic work. At the piano, Brian was able to immerse himself in a world that he could relate to, a world of both safety and adventure. Music also provided another bond with his mother, who was more than happy to sing and play with him.

The Wilson family piano was located in a converted garage, which was known as the music room, alongside Audree's Hammond organ. As the three brothers began to outgrow their shared bedroom, Brian took up residence in the music room. He now could play as late as he wanted, so long as Murry was in a good humour.

As Brian, Dennis and Carl grew older, the scope for family music making increased, although Dennis showed some reluctance to join in. He escaped whenever possible, as his own clashes with Murry quickly became the most heated and violent within the sometime dysfunctional household. Dennis wanted to be close to his father, but father and son were both too confrontational and aggressive to keep their relationship on an even keel. Dennis sang with his brothers in their shared bedroom, but this was usually the extent of his involvement. Later, in his mid-teens, Dennis would find pleasure in the piano, and his suggestion that his brothers sing a song about surfing would ignite their musical career. In the meantime, Carl, who idolised his oldest brother, happily joined Brian and Audree in singing and playing. Carl was initially attracted to the violin as played by Spade Cooley on singing cowboy television shows, but he soon switched his enthusiasm to the guitar.

Brian's childhood musical influences were many and various. Gershwin's "Rhapsody in Blue" was an early touchstone. Brian first heard this piece at a very young age, and sensed in it a way of expressing complex emotions through music. Indeed, Beach Boys' writer Andrew Doe once described witnessing Brian in a studio in the eighties – a time when his emotional and physical health were at a low ebb – playing the whole of Gershwin's magnificent piece without speaking to anyone. "Rhapsody in Blue" had become an emotional anchor for Brian: an expression of the power of music to touch the deepest reaches of his being. Brian still carries a CD copy of the piece as essential luggage today.

Another key early influence on Brian was the vocal harmony group The Four Freshmen. After catching their jazz-influenced harmonising on the radio, Brian rushed to a record store, disappearing into a booth with *The Four Freshmen and Five Trombones*. Back at home, the record rotated on the family turntable for weeks, and soon more Four Freshman discs were echoing around the Wilson house.

Brian replayed Four Freshman cuts again and again in order to work out the different harmony lines. He then taught the parts to his younger brothers. The Four Freshman provided Brian with an emotional as well as a music education, as he revealed to *Performing Songwriter* years later, "I was so into the sound of the harmonies," he said, "that I learned how to be happy from that album."

Brian also enjoyed The Four Preps and The Hi-Los, while school music lessons exposed him to choral and orchestral music. However, as Brian

© Capitol Photo Archives

*Albums typical of Brian's taste.*

began spending more time with Mike Love, his cousin would expand his musical horizons beyond sonatas and innocent white pop by introducing him to R & B.

Los Angeles in the late fifties was a jazz and R&B town at the street and club level, with a steady proliferation of small independent labels augmenting the three bigger companies, ABC Paramount, Capitol and MGM. Small local labels like Del-Fi provided a wealth of earthy radio fodder for the baby boomers. Local groups like Little Caesar and The Romans, The Cadets, The Flairs, The Gallahads and The Pentagons were required wireless listening for L.A. youth, along with national faves like The Penguins, The Mystics, and Frankie Lymon & The Teenagers.

L.A. radio was divided into distinct black and white stations. The big white station was KFWB, which, along with KDAY, played "polite, no-groove music" according to Bruce Johnston. The main black station was KGFJ, which featured DJs like Hunter Hancock and Huggie Boy spinning serious R&B. Mike Love's groove came from this more radical output. The influence on Brian is evident in the similarity of "Help Me Rhonda" to Buster Brown's old number, "Fannie Mae."

Brian and Mike also regularly tuned into the Johnny Otis Show on KVOX; Otis's choice of discs increased Brian's awareness of more harmonious forms of pop. Otis also hosted a weekly TV show, which gave young white kids one of their first chances to experience the power of black R&B artists like James Brown.

On Brian's sixteenth birthday, his parents bought him a Woolensack tape recorder. This opened up a new world of musical possibilities to the young musician. Brian was delighted when he realised he and his mum Audree could put their own two singing parts on top of two previously recorded ones, and made his first attempts at over-dubbing.

Brian's parents approved of his developing music ambition, but as he grew into his later teens, Murry became increasingly frustrated that his oldest son was not going to be the first-team sports player he desired. Brian performed sports adequately, but was clearly never going to achieve top jock status. While Audree valued her son's "gentle soul," Murry would goad Brian with taunts of "namby-pamby". As for his brothers, Dennis was physically outgoing but dysfunctional in school, and sought his outlets in more hedonistic pursuits, while Carl was the "baby" who grew to be the family diplomat, and suffered less pressure than his older brothers because he was the youngest.

Family tension aside, Brian maintained a lively sense of humour that helped him gain acceptance among his peers. He began to socialise at local hang-outs like The 'Wich Stand, the sort of meeting spot that he would later write about in "Fun, Fun, Fun." When Brian reached the car-owning stage shortly after Mike Love, he found himself spending more and more time with his older cousin. The two of them would sit up at night in Brian's car listening to radio stations like Hollywood's mainstream KFWB, occasions later recalled by Mike in the intro to his song, "Brian's Back." Brian's increased mobility allowed him to widen his musical circle, taking part in school musical gatherings, as well as harmonising with Mike and his sister Maureen, on hits of the day like "In The Still Of The Night."

Mike Love graduated from Dorsey High in 1958 and started working in the family business, eventually also taking a job pumping gas. Before long, Mike got his High School girlfriend pregnant and married her. This set Mike apart from Brian to an extent, and allowed him to lord his sexual prowess over his more inexperienced cousin. The difference in the two young men's singing voices would accentuate such rivalry.

Brian was impressed with the way Mike's bass singing sounded against his own much higher ranges. Brian's own voice was in the high alto range, and he had the ability to sing sweetly and richly in falsetto, a skill he developed singing his mother's favourite Rosemary Clooney songs for her. However, Brian's high voice made him even more insecure about his masculinity, especially when comparing himself to the bass bragadaccio of his cousin. Plagued with doubts about his abilities to cut it in the manly world of sports, Brian was often embarrassed to sing in such an unmasculine style. On one occasion he arrived home from High School in floods of tears after his singing had resulted in taunts of "cissy". The subsequent use of his highest range would always be a double-edged sword for Brian, and much later his wife Marilyn recalled how much self-doubt it had given rise to.

✳ ✳ ✳ ✳ ✳ ✳

By the summer of 1961, with records like Shep & The Limelites' "Daddy's Home" and The Regents' "Barbara Ann" riding high in the U.S. Hot 100, Brian was studying psychology ("to understand more about how people think") at El Camino Junior College. It was there that he met Al Jardine, on the school football team.

Like Brian, Al was more interested in music than football, though his preference was for the folk music scene. At Brian's behest, Al began to join in with the singing sessions he was regularly holding with Mike and Maureen Love and his brother Carl. As Maureen dropped out, Brian, Mike, Carl and Al became a more regular grouping, and began to form the core of what would become The Beach Boys.

## Chapter 2
# IT'S BEEN BUILDING UP INSIDE OF ME...:
## THE MUSICAL JOURNEY TOWARDS *PET SOUNDS*

*"My father was critical of the first thing we did."*
— Brian Wilson (on "Surfin'")

*"There was a natural creativity with Brian...recording techniques evolved which allowed us to stretch out even more in terms of sound textures. Brian took advantage of that and pioneered his way through."*
— Mike Love

After early recording experiments with his Woolensack recording machine, Brian graduated to a local studio in mid-1961. An early session with Al Jardine and a couple of friends led to Brian, Al, Mike and Carl returning to cut a version of a song called "Surfin'" – written on the suggestion of the only surfing Wilson boy, Dennis.

The studio's owners, Hite and Dorinda, were so impressed that they had the boys re-record the song at the Stereo Masters Studio in Hollywood and had it issued on the tiny Candix label that Autumn. The record soon began to pick up local airplay and for Brian the thrill of hearing his own record on the radio was unrivalled. The single went on to reach number 75 on the national charts and then sank without trace – probably due to the small label's inability to fund a potential hit.

By February 1962, the boys had been re-named The Beach Boys by Russ Regan, the distributor for their Candix release. Regan was discussing the group with West Coast producer Joe Saraceno and wanted to come up with a moniker that fitted with their surf-themed material. Under their new name they recorded three more tracks with Hite Morgan, including two songs with the same theme as their debut: "Surfin' Safari" and "Surfer Girl". However, before the new material could be released, Candix went into liquidation and the boys were once again without a label.

In the meantime, the success of "Surfin'" had attracted considerable interest. Budding local songwriter Gary Usher was one of those impressed by The Beach Boys' talent, and he showed up at the Wilson home to meet

Brian. Before long Usher had become Brian's first proper writing partner, and Brian has often given Usher credit for teaching him everything he knows about writing songs. "He showed me how to write around chords, play chords on the guitar and write songs," Brian explained to *Performing Songwriter* magazine in 1996. "He wrote both melody and words. He was really up and it turned me on and I started writing songs on my own. But he had to teach me first about how to get that spirit going."

The first song Brian and Gary collaborated on was "Lonely Sea" which took Brian's writing into new emotional territory. They also worked on a song called "409", which Dennis – having rejoined the group at Audree's insistence – was particularly keen on. With these two songs, and plans for re-recorded versions of "Surfin' Safari" and "Judy", Brian and the group relocated to Sunset Boulevard's Western Studios – a professional set-up where many hit singers of the day had already recorded. It became a hugely important learning experience for Brian. Chuck Britz, the engineer on those sessions, recalled that, "on those first cuts at Western, a great deal of time was spent by me teaching Brian *and* Murry about the studio!

"That first session was really me tolerating a lot of Brian," Britz explained, "and tolerating a lot of Murry, because neither one of them really knew anything about the studio, and, of course, Murry was alienated because I was showing him up and teaching Brian things. Murry was always pretending he knew things even though he didn't. He just had no idea what was going on, and Brian knew that as well."

Chuck Britz would become Brian's recording mentor for the next four years. Brian had experienced four different smaller studios in a very short time, and was now very eager to learn from the first real expert he had encountered.

With fresh recordings completed, a conflict developed between Murry Wilson and Gary Usher. Usher was keen to shop the tapes around his music business contacts, but Murry insisted that he get first shot, and managed to arrange a meeting with Capitol Records through Russ Regan. Capitol was a large staid company looking to increase its virtually non-existent youth catalogue. The label had recently recruited former pop singer Nick Venet to spot promising talent. Venet's main interest was in securing a local act to rival white New York Doo Wop acts such as Dion And The Belmonts and The Mystics, but he was excited by Brian's arrangements and The Beach Boys' youthful sound, and signed them immediately. The band was then sent to Capitol's studio to re-record their early songs.

For The Beach Boys' first single, Capitol saw "409" as the A-side of a coupling with "Surfin' Safari" on the basis that it would have wider appeal across the market. Meanwhile, further changes had taken place in The Beach

*Nick Venet's EP cover reflects the safer, white side of Rock & Roll.*

Boys camp: unconvinced of any future after the first "Surfin'" hit, Al Jardine had left the group. Al's replacement was a young and inexperienced neighbourhood friend of Carl's called David Marks who was drafted in on rhythm guitar.

The five-piece Beach Boys line-up of Brian, Mike, Dennis, Carl and David soon enjoyed a string of hits, beginning with the June 1962 release of the third version of "Surfin' Safari," which was the song that made Capitol realise surf music could be widely marketable. By August, the group had hurriedly recorded their first album at Capitol's Hollywood studio. Though Gary Usher was not a part of the group, he had co-writer credits for six of Brian's songs.

The band's debut album *Surfin' Safari* set the tone for Beach Boys output over the next three years or so. Mike was the main lead singer on all the up-beat teen-oriented tracks, and Brian initially kept a comparatively low profile with only one solo lead on the first album. This increased to three on the second album *Surfin' USA*, released in March '63, well before the title track became the boys' hottest hit to date as it peaked in the Top 3 at the end of May. Brian's three lead vocals were most significant, coming as they did on songs that would mark the beginning of Brian's shift away from the band's "fun in the sun" subject matter.

One of Brian's most telling lead vocal excursions on the *Surfin' USA* album was the Wilson/Usher ballad "Lonely Sea". Sad and plaintive in feel, it was the first Beach Boys track to show a flipside to the bright summer fun.

According to band associate and ex-Sunray Rick Henn, this song, though a primitive example of Brian's work, remained Murry's favourite ever. With its gentle evocation of sunset and seascape, Brian sung comfortably within his alto range, holding long clear notes. Brian also employed an unusual device for the group (though it was common enough then in pop) of a spoken section to talk of the "pain in my heart", in what was Brian's first real musical exposure of his emotions. The background vocals cover the whole range, with Brian's falsetto defining the lovely fading tag. Similarly, *Surfin' USA*'s "Farmer's Daughter" and "Lana" are both led by Brian's falsetto, soaring confidently above the group's mid-range backing vocals.

"'Farmers Daughter' was my first chance to fully prove I had a good falsetto voice," Brian recalled years later. "I don't have a macho kind of sound in my throat, but I'm proud of my sound."

However, it was "Lana", featuring a xylophone duplicating the guitar line to produce a new sweet sound, which gave an important pointer to what was to come musically… "Brian was fooling around with The Beach Boys sound at that time…trying to alter it," nominal producer Nick Venet told Californian music historian Stephen McParland in 1997. "I don't think he knew how to do it yet, but he did know he wanted to change it. He was experimenting…"

By early 1963, The Beach Boys had relocated to Western Recorders studios. Realising that both the surf and car songs were selling separately, Capitol put pressure on Brian for more soundalike product. Brian was already working at quite a pace, keeping up with his writing and recording and the new demands of live shows. By now he had little time for anything that could be described as regular life.

Continuing the surf/car singles pairing plan, "Surfer Girl" b/w "Little Deuce Coupe" hit in Summer 1963, both breaking the U.S. Top 20. "Surfer Girl," which exhibited wonderful chord changes, was Brian's first full production. The hit version was considerably richer in vocal and production texture than the earlier Hite Morgan version. All the constituents now combined to produce a richer Beach Boys sound light years beyond the disposable feel of their debut album.

In September, Capitol rushed out an album called *Surfer Girl*, a mixture of rollicking songs and pretty ballads following the surf theme. Brian has professed delight at the production on "Catch A Wave"'s vocals, and "Little Deuce Coupe"'s rhythm. The album also saw him showing an increasing confidence with his falsetto range. Meanwhile, Brian was able to bring out the widest variety in Mike's untutored nasal bass ranges which best fitted the group's more commercial pop sides. Mike was more than happy to develop into the group's on-stage frontman, a job to which his outgoing personality was supremely suited. Nonetheless, it was Brian who was acknowledged as the group's leader. Murry ensured that contractually Brian had the right to hire and fire band members as he saw fit. Unsurprisingly, Brian seemed only to want to take the lead on musical matters, and shied away from other potential areas of conflict. Indeed, on a later live appearance on Britain's famous *Ready Steady Go* TV programme Brian appeared reluctant to acknowledge his status. When asked if he was the leader during group introductions, he murmured uncomfortably, "Yeah, I guess I am."

*The Surfer Girl* album featured one of the songs that most acutely portrayed Brian's introspective nature, "In My Room". While Mike Love faced any disagreement with defiance, Brian would withdraw to his room on occasions of conflict or sadness. Written with Gary Usher, "In My Room" was the natural successor to "Surfer Girl" in terms of overall sound and feel, but its lyrical content exposed Brian's sensitivity and emotional fragility. It was the sort of private song that other musicians might have been reluctant to release, but for Brian it was such an eloquent, and possibly cathartic, portrayal of his emotional world that he could not have left it off the record. When Brian and Gary finished writing the song late one night at the Wilson home, they played it straight away to Murry and Audree, and to Brian's delight it met with their immediate acclaim. Brian, who always searched for approval from those around him, must have been overjoyed to receive immediate praise from his parents.

In the summer of 1963, Brian began to reach out beyond the confines of The Beach Boys. On June 14th, he ventured into Phil Spector's favourite studio, the more pop-orientated Gold Star, to record two tracks. For "Back Home" and "Black Wednesday" (the working title for Sharon Marie's "Runaround Lover") Brian used five of Spector's legendary collection of musicians later known as "The Wrecking Crew": David Gates, Jay Migliori, Steve Douglas, Carol Kaye and Hal Blaine. Brian would employ roughly the same set of musicians later that year for "outside" productions for The Honeys, Paul Peterson and The Survivors, and gradually involved them increasingly frequently on actual Beach Boys' tracks. All but Gates would later form the nucleus of musicians with which Brian would build the *Pet Sounds* tracks.

The use of Spector's studio and sideman was no accident. Spector was a key touchstone for Brian Wilson. As Brian was dipping his first tentative toe into the music business, Phil Spector was already the hot young producer in town having been apprenticed to the experienced Leiber and Stoller in New York. Upon his arrival in Los Angeles, Spector had begun to fully develop his trademark "Wall Of Sound" which so captivated the young Brian. This found its full force with what would become Brian's all-time favourite record, The Ronettes' "Be My Baby", and it was not long before he sought to visit Spector at work at Gold Star. It seemed to Brian that Spector was really rolling back the boundaries of production techniques, with his brash massed instrumental combinations, during which he cajoled the hard core of session players to tear up the rule book. Brian was continually fascinated with Spector's productions, initially seeking to copy them with the later Honeys' work, but soon to integrate some of Spector's ideas of percussion, echo and combinations into his own developing work. Over the following years, Brian would remain aware of Spector's stature as a competitive reference point as well as retaining his straight-forward admiration of Spector's work. The links via the session musicians also served as an ongoing reminder for Brian of the "producer on the pedestal" that Spector had become to him. However, as Brian's work took on its own cohesive new directions, the spectre of Spector lessened as Brian became more confident with his own recordings.

Back in Beach Boys' territory, Capitol Records maintained their intensive marketing policy by putting out a car-themed collection entitled *Little Deuce Coupe* only one month after the release of *Surfer Girl*. While the new album shared two songs with its surf-oriented predecessor, it was a strong collection in its own right. All the songs were now taking on a richer sound, and the newer group vocals sounded more mature.

By this point Brian had a new lyric collaborator in Roger Christian, a local radio DJ and a car lover with a good grip of hip vernacular and hot rod slang. Christian wrote half of this new car album, submitting completed lyrics for Brian to set to music – a different way of working to the more fluid Usher collaborations. In contrast to the introspection of "In My Room", *Little Deuce Coupe* saw an unmistakably macho feel creeping into the band's lyrics and music, reflecting Brian and the boys' growing confidence. Brian even tried Dion's cool street swagger for "Car Crazy Cutie". Brian also engaged in confident falsetto workouts on "Spirit Of America" and "No-Go Showboat". The group vocals are showcased on two tracks, "Ballad Of Ole Betsy" and the older Bobby Troup song, "A Young Man Is Gone."

"The way the voices fitted together was very complex," Jimmy Webb noted of the latter track in a reissue sleevenote. "The voices all lie down beside each other very easily; there's no bumping between the voices because the pitch is very precise. Everybody knows the pitch, and they would sing it and do it until they got it right."

This was an extremely creative time for Brian and one of his happiest times musically. In just two years since his first tentative steps into a recording studio Brian was largely responsible for four hit albums, over a dozen singles and a Number 1 hit song, "Surf City," which he had given away to Jan & Dean – much to Murry's chagrin. Murry knew his son wanted to break out from the confines of The Beach Boys, and was keen to ensure that he remained loyal to the family's career chances. However, with close involvement in a number-one hit, Brian now felt confident enough to follow his own muse.

1964 was a momentous year for Brian. The previous year, he had broken up with his first serious girlfriend, Judy Bowles, and met Marilyn Rovell through Gary Usher. Brian married Marilyn later in the year, and very soon afterwards suffered the breakdown that caused his withdrawal from touring with The Beach Boys. The pressures of writing, recording and touring simply proved too much. However, the breakdown would bring with it a benefit. At this stage Brian had opportunities that had long been denied to him. He could stay and work at home and keep more regular hours, compared to the punishing touring schedule followed by the other Beach Boys. Away from the pressures of life on the road, Brian had more of a chance to set his own work agenda. However, the breakdown had exposed psychological weaknesses and caused him to deeply question his already erratic self-confidence. Knowing that he had been knocked over left a potentially open wound, but removed from the immediate pressures of the touring band he was able to take stock, re-sort his priorities, and realise his mounting desire to move towards deeper, richer Beach Boys music.

Brian's first musical release of 1964 – in January, on Capitol – saw him once again drawing on the talents of Spector's musicians. "Pamela Jean" by The Survivors was a re-write of "Car Crazy Cutie" from the *Little Deuce Coupe* album, with elements of his Gary Usher and Roger Christian collaboration "Muscle Beach Party" thrown in. Recorded by Brian and his friends Bob Norberg, Dave Nowlen and Rich Alarian, the song did not sell, and quickly became one of the most collectable of Brian's records. Of more interest, however, was the flip side, "After The Game". This gentle instrumental showed Brian experimenting with the guitar as lead instrument and featured a pretty and rounded sound that would lead to the picked guitar figure on "Don't Worry Baby" and on to the musical mood of *Pet Sounds*. "After The Game" also featured a woodblock-type sound that Brian made by hitting a chair with a stick, punctuating the steady brushed snare rhythm. Around the same time Brian discovered drummer Hal Blaine's famed "box of tricks" – a wide range of different percussive sounds – which further fuelled his enthusiasm for the more unusual percussion combinations that soon became a hallmark of Brian Wilson productions.

*A rare instrumental B-side, produced by Brian apart from The Beach Boys.*

The first two Beach Boys albums of the year, *Shut Down Vol.2* and *All Summer Long*, continued the band's successful formula. Each contained some standard genre songs, some filler tracks, and some classic Brian Wilson.

Much of *Shut Down Vol.2* is fairly standard teen fare of the kind Brian could quickly hammer out without too much effort. However, three songs on the record do stand out as steps to greater things. The lovely ballad "Keep An Eye On Summer" finds Brian coming to terms with a lost love and features fine harmonies behind his lead. "The Warmth Of The Sun," written by Brian and Mike at Capitol's offices the night of Kennedy's assassination, continues with a similar melancholy feel.

"We were just playing around with a very light chord thing, from C to Am7 to E flat and Cm7, which I thought was a great new chord pattern," Brian later told *Performing Songwriter* magazine, before going on to explain the key to his melody writing. "Get behind the chords," he said, "The further behind the chords you get, the more melodic you can be. Behind meaning concentrate more and put all your eggs into the melody."

Both of these moody ballads worked great as album tracks, however Brian's third instant-classic on the record, "Don't Worry Baby," had all the prerequisites for a single. Supposedly written with The Ronettes in mind, but apparently rejected by Phil Spector, the song has become one of the most enduring and most covered of any in the Beach Boys canon. Brian's lead voice on the original is more confident than ever, and the arrangement blends all his guitar, percussive and vocal developments into one glorious

© Capitol Photo Archives

whole. All of this notwithstanding, "Don't Worry Baby" only saw a 45 rpm release as the B-side to "I Get Around," which told the story of the group and showcased Brian and the band at their commercial best. "Don't Worry Baby", on the other hand, was a big step in the alternative direction Brian was pursuing on his own.

The recording of the A-side also illustrated a key difference between Brian and Mike Love's musical sensibilities. "I Get Around" originally began with a Brian-arranged full Four Freshman-style harmony. Mike was unsure of it, and suggested that they cut straight to the famed "*Round, round, get around*" intro. This was solid commercial thinking as such an ear-catching opening was sure to maximise radio play. Meanwhile over in Britain, people were actually picking up on the B-side alongside the hit song – a very rare event in those days – giving a swell of positive British interest in Brian's new direction from the start. The two sides of this single, encapsulate the two poles of Beach Boys music in 1964: the instantly popular fizzing pop concoction of "I Get Around", against the maturing wine of "Don't Worry Baby," which, while initially less accessible, demonstrated a deeper imagination and beauty.

When the *All Summer Long* album was released in mid-1964, it was immediately obvious that Brian had achieved one of his objectives: he had moved the album's theme away from the limited strictures of surf and car songs. There were now wider lyrical themes of young life and love. Brian was cruising faster towards his goals, even though they almost certainly weren't yet fully formed in his mind.

During the group's hectic period of early hits, something else occurred to deeply influence Brian. Britain's music charts were already filled with Beatles music and other beat boom groups. Taking a broad spread of influences from American music, The Beatles easily won over Britain, but this victory was far less significant than their full-on conquering of the U.S. charts. The Beach Boys and The Four Seasons were the only mainstream white U.S. pop groups to really withstand the onslaught and keep having major hits amid the massive wave to buy practically anything British. Had Brian not already extended his group's material beyond the surf and car roots, The Beach Boys too would have almost certainly been washed away. Brian's competitive edge began to show, especially when The Beatles settled on Capitol as their main U.S. outlet.

*All Summer Long* was released a few weeks after The Beatles had smashed the singles charts, and Brian was well aware of the threat the Fab Four posed. The new Beach Boys album had a fine set of songs, many of which could have been hit singles. The up-tempo songs like "All Summer Long", "Little Honda", "Drive-In" (the first time Brian used a dramatic dead stop in a track), "Do You Remember" and "Don't Back Down" (the final surf song) all evoked different aspects of American late teen summers. To balance these, Brian revisited a late Doo Wop favourite with a lovely version of The Mystics' "Hushabye" and brought out another Wilson/Usher song "We'll Run Away" that followed the thread of romantic introspection originating from "In My Room" and "The Warmth Of the Sun". Brian's most progressive creations on the album, "Wendy" and "Girls On The Beach," represent a maturing view of the opposite sex. "Wendy" begins with the most striking of guitar intros, giving no clue as to what is to follow until the combined voices enter. The chords on "Wendy" are comparatively simple, whereas those on "Girls On The Beach" are much wider ranging, with the addition of a wonderful short bridge. The final track is the rocker "Don't Back Down", in which the macho surfer lyrics could easily be transposed onto the growing rivalry that Brian perceived between himself and The Beatles.

Capitol Records released two more Beach Boys albums that year: *The Beach Boys' Christmas Album* and *Beach Boys' Concert*. The Christmas album brought Brian into contact with conductor Dick Reynolds and his orchestra. The following year, Brian would work with Reynolds as part of his recording preparations for *Pet Sounds*. In fact, some of the same string players would also play under Brian's direction for the actual *Pet Sounds* sessions. The *Concert* album collected Beach Boys hits with other favourites from the early sixties. More importantly, this period marked a growing willingness for Brian to make fundamental alterations to previous recordings. "Little Saint Nick", "Little Honda" and "Don't Back Down" all exist in substantially different versions, as opposed to the simpler lyrical re-writes on "Pamela Jean". At this point Brian entered an intense period of self-scrutiny as his self-imposed standards continued to rise. When all of the pressures on Brian to keep writing hits and touring constantly came to a head at Christmas 1964, it was extremely concerning. However it gave Brian more time at home, and allowed him to further develop his writing and recording techniques.

Brian's personality had several sides. The competitiveness from his school sports days was now translated into musical ambition. Although he was polite and good-humoured, he was emotionally more fragile than many people around him. Normal social growth and life skills had been stunted by his full-time involvement with The Beach Boys; Brian had simply never had the time to be an ordinary young man. According to David Marks, Brian's coping strategy on the road was to ignore the people around him and withdraw to his hotel room.

*A rare 7" juke box EP to promote the* Today *album.*

Brian's comparative introspection surfaced on 1965's *The Beach Boys Today*, which, more than any other record, points the way toward *Pet Sounds*. The whole album reflects his growing studio mastery and inventiveness, and is usually characterised as having a slow side and a fast side, with the latter being closer to traditional Beach Boys' territory.

Despite the usual received wisdom that Brian needed a good lyricist, *The Beach Boys Today* includes soulful, emotional lyrics penned by Brian himself. In the context of The Beach Boys' thematic evolution, *Today* represents an emergence from adolescence into adulthood. "When I Grow Up (To Be A Man)" is a perfect example of Brian's examination of a young man's life, as he realises he is leaving his youth behind. Meanwhile, more mature comparisons between girls and women are made in "Don't Hurt My Little Sister."

"Please Let Me Wonder," "Kiss Me Baby" and "She Knows Me So Well" form the album's romantic trilogy. With these cuts, Brian appears totally immersed and confident in his craft – a man who has moved forward in his relationships but retains his tenderness. "Please Let Me Wonder" is especially illustrative of Brian's maturing instrumental themes, with its heavy plucking on the bass becoming the main driving motif, and droning saxes underpinning the song. The group's harmonies, ever richer and more complex throughout the album, are at their peak on these songs. "Kiss Me Baby" has a wonderful melody, and one of the most complicated set of background vocals Brian had yet attempted.

"One song that was important working towards Pet Sounds was 'She Knows Me Too Well'," Brian explains. "Also 'In The Back Of My Mind', which was the heaviest – it was very deep, lyrically and musically."

Though carrying a Mike Love co-writing credit, the former describes the protective caress of Brian's relationship with Marilyn, and shows that he had the fully formed musical palate to vividly represent deep emotions. The album's penultimate track is the sparser and jazz-tinged "In The Back Of My Mind," which features Dennis on lead. Brian's experiments with new orchestration appear here, and his ideas with the strings set up a template for further work. Bruce Johnston points to this track as a precursor to Pet Sounds, "That track was a great creative dark traffic jam. It is dark and confusing, and begged the question as to why it was on that album. Listen to that one particularly."

The album closes with another "talkie" track, "Bull Session With Big Daddy" during which the group discusses life on the road on the autumn 1964 European trip. One notable moment comes when Brian claims "I've never made a mistake in my life." Mike immediately responds that they are all waiting for him to make one. Read into that what you will.

A notable out-take from the Today sessions was "Guess I'm Dumb" which is assumed to have been conceived as a Beach Boys release, although it ended up as a one-off Capitol single by session guitarist, and temporary Beach Boy, Glen Campbell. Its arrangement displays all the musical elements that Brian was working with at the time: punctuating trumpets, trombones and saxes, and strings behind the break. The saxes featured a raspy bass drone effect that Brian was to use more extensively on Pet Sounds, either in sax, harmonica or accordion form. The strings provided an extra and unifying wrap that lifts the track towards the end, while percussion added to the heavy bass and floor tom gave extra density. Bongos filled regular spaces, while the descending bass lines featured a delightful glissando effect reminiscent of Phil Spector. With only minimal background vocals, the recording is unlike any other Beach Boys' track to that date, which may explain why a group vocal version has not been uncovered. Campbell's expressive vocal is good on a song that is hard to sing well, but one that has attracted several interesting covers over the years. Although not a Beach Boys' release, it was nevertheless a distinct further step for Brian in forming the instrumental blends and combinations that he would use on *Pet Sounds*.

"That was important with the feels in the music," Brian recently recalled. "It was very like a Burt Bacharach kind of thing."

Brian was already aware of Burt's sophisticated talents and command of unpredictable melodic structure – indeed "Guess I'm Dumb" borrows melodically from Burt's "Walk On By" – and Burt's influence was another catalyst in Brian's drive to compete in the pop marketplace.

Hot on the heels of *Today*, with Capitol's policy of mid-year Beach Boys blitzing, came the *Summer Days (And Summer Nights!!)* album. It would turn out to be the last formula offering. Only three of the tracks were single A-sides, but another four could easily have gained that status. "You're So Good To Me" in particular, with its blazing Leslie'd guitar lead, should have been a British A-side. At any party at the time in London, this track was the hottest favourite with its simple but storming chorus. "California Girls," "Then I Kissed Her" (a U.K. single release) and a re-vamped "Help Me Rhonda", with tightened up vocals and new guitar part, were the hits in the package. Bruce Johnston especially values the adventurous symphonic intro to "California Girls," the first Beach Boys recording that he sung on. Together with other strong tracks like "The Girl From New York City," "Amusement Parks USA" and "Salt Lake City," the hits tended to overshadow the two tracks which are now especially revered by lovers of the Brian Wilson thread of musical development. "Girl Don't Tell Me" was Carl Wilson's first credited lead vocal on a gentle song written by Brian. Its simplicity serves as a counterbalance to the much fuller tracks around it. "Let Him Run Wild" was also notable for its tempo and mood shifts; techniques which Brian would go on to develop extensively.

The last three tracks continued the group's run of odd album endings with an instrumental, another bit of nonsense, and a beautiful group a capella. The guitar-led instrumental, "Summer Means New Love", was impressionistic and melancholy – though drawing on a wide palette of sounds. After the nonsense of "I'm Bugged At My Old Man," Brian's ill-disguised dig at Murry (who was comparatively estranged from Brian at this point) came "And Your Dreams Come True", which was a beautiful example of Brian's masterful skill in arranging the group's vocal blend.

Brian's increasing boldness was also shown in a non-album single release in November 1965 of "The Little Girl I Once Knew." The song featured wonderfully complex harmonies and several long complete pauses. Consequently it was disliked by radio stations and charted poorly. To compensate, Capitol quickly issued "Barbara Ann" from *The Beach Boys Party* – a quickly recorded singalong album, which, though unrepresentative of Brian's musical maturity, did pay homage to many of the band's shared early and current musical influences. "Barbara Ann" was a huge hit everywhere, and certainly convinced many at Capitol that, whilst Brian's experimentation was interesting enough, there was nothing to beat a solid, simple, unashamed commercial hit. Meanwhile, Brian's drive towards new standards for the group meant that he was also setting higher goals for the instrumental details of each track. Before *Pet Sounds* was to arrive, Capitol expected another single, and the strongest work-in-progress was "Sloop John B". Brian could hear a possible improvement to the existing track, and went to some incredible lengths to change the sound. Guitarist Billy Strange explains:

"I vividly remember him calling me in on a Sunday morning just after Christmas 1965 to over-dub the solo on 'Sloop John B.' I told him I couldn't make it because of having my son that weekend… Brian convinced me to come by the studio anyway and listen to the track. I thought that I would be called in later to over-dub. Between the time he called and I arrived, Brian had called a music store-owner in Hollywood, had him open his store and purchased an electric twelve string and amplifier for me to use on the tune. I arrived at Western #1 and began listening to the track. After setting up the amp and tuning the guitar, I played a sixteen bar solo, *one time*, and Brian said, 'That's a take, go home.' As I was getting ready to leave, Brian gave me five $100.00 bills, and said 'Don't forget to take your guitar and amp with you.' He made me a gift of several hundred dollars worth of guitar and amplifier. Plus paying me an exorbitant fee for the session!"

Brian's ability to know instinctively the sounds that were right for his work was reaching its absolute peak, and despite the seemingly retrogressive step of the *Party* album, he was ready to lift The Beach Boys' music onto a new plateau. Brian's former wife distinctly remembers him telling her one night around this time, "Marilyn, I'm gonna make the greatest album ever made."

After eleven previous albums for Capitol, and still only 23 years old, Brian was ready to make his masterpiece.

# Chapter 3
## THE UNBRIDLED ROAR OF ENTHUSIASM:
## THE WRITING OF *PET SOUNDS*

*Tony Asher in 1965.*

*"Brian's thing was music, not words, and I think he felt a little unsure of himself in that area. I, on the other hand, was a 'word person'...he recognised that and very likely called me in on the project for that very reason."*
　　　　　　　　　　　　　　　　　　　　　　　　　　　　– Tony Asher

*"The words of Tony Asher blended into the melodic slices of Wilson, spoke of the pain and coming of age that allowed all ambitious dudes to let him speak for us whilst we hid whatever and hung tough."*
　　　　　　　　　　　　　　　　　　– Andrew Loog Oldham (Manager/producer)

*One of Brian's srongest outside productions.*

By mid 1965, 23-year-old Brian Wilson had written or co-written in excess of 80 released songs for The Beach Boys, and several others for acts like The Honeys, Sharon Marie, The Survivors and The Castells. He had worked collaboratively with Mike Love, Gary Usher, Roger Christian, Russ Titelman ("Guess I'm Dumb"), Bob Norberg and a little with brother Carl and Al Jardine. Received opinion had it that Brian needed a lyrical collaborator, although the high standard of his most recent solo compositions on albums like *Today* had shown that this was far from essential. Brian did however see himself predominately as the composer of the music, and may have sometimes found the exact placing and shaping of lyrics a chore.

Early Beach Boys lyrics about surfing and cars were celebrations of youthful hedonism. However, such simple ideas, expressed in straightforward forms, though commercially desirable, no longer satisfied Brian. While his thoughts and pre-occupations were often those of any eager young man, Brian's recent experience of the contrary forces of extreme external pressure and extreme cosseting from the outside world had a profound effect on him. The elder Wilson boy was a "sensitive soul", as his mother described him, and recent pressures exacerbated his already poor ability to deal with the emotional turmoil of life in The Beach Boys.

A number of Brian's more mature recent songs had shown the gradual emergence of a more sensitive side, as he rejected hot dogging and hot rodding in favour of writing about his own emotional experience. It was as if Brian's public acclaim had given him the confidence to open up his soul. Like Motown's de facto New Man, Smokey Robinson, Brian appeared unafraid to let his feminine side show.

By the summer of 1965, despite Brian's withdrawal from the rigours of touring, he was still suffering from the continuing pressure from Capitol to deliver the next proper studio album. The *Party* album was a quick stop-gap. The fact that it had produced a huge hit was an added bonus, but there was no escaping Capitol's insistence that the next proper Beach Boys album was overdue. Meanwhile, Brian continued to procrastinate, sensing that he was almost within reach of the body of music what would encompass his expanded vision and top the work of his hero Phil Spector.

"Musically I'm still searching for a new thing, a new bag, a new field," Brian told a journalist at the time. "I don't know what's coming, but I know what's here. The Dylan cult is now a realisation, and other than that – things like the Phil Spector approach to production, and the Burt Bacharach style of writing."

Searching around for a lyrical collaborator who could write words to match his increasing maturity with his grand musical ambitions, Brian asked his friend Loren Schwartz for advice. He suggested a young advertising executive called Tony Asher.

Brian was already familiar with Asher, having briefly met him at one of Loren's parties earlier that summer. Shortly afterwards, Asher happened upon Brian at a recording studio. During a break the two young men exchanged musical thoughts, and before they went their separate ways, Asher played a couple of song ideas to Brian.

British-born Asher had moved with his family to Los Angeles at an early age, and during his college years had enjoyed musical collaborations with Kelly Gordon (who wrote Sinatra's "That's Life") and Tommy Oliver, and formed a long lasting friendship with the future arranger Perry Botkin Jr. A handsome young bachelor who had trained as a journalist, Asher was working for the popular Carson-Roberts advertising agency when he met Brian. Asher had a strong musical background – at one point he had even considered playing jazz piano for a living – and had quickly become an accomplished jingle writer. Like most of young California, he was a big fan of the Beach Boys, so it was particularly thrilling for him to meet Brian.

"Brian called me and explained that he was overdue in delivering to the label," Asher recalls. "He was frustrated as he said that he had an image of a new body of work. He said he couldn't imagine writing it with anyone he already knew – not any of his previous collaborators. He knew he had to find the right person."

During mid-autumn of 1965, Brian invited Asher over to his house to discuss a possible collaboration. Unfortunately, when Asher arrived at the appointed time, there was no sign of Brian. Phone calls were exchanged and this initially unsettling hurdle overcome, the two of them reconvened and Asher was thrilled to find himself being seriously considered for the position.

"I was awe-struck!" he remembers. "I was a great fan of Brian's, but oddly I wasn't intimidated. I wasn't sure why I wasn't trembling! But I was really worried that we wouldn't have anything to say." In fact, the pair struck up an easy and honest friendship, and Brian decided that Asher was the man for the job.

Asher immediately arranged a three-week leave of absence from his advertising job and the pair embarked on discussions about the album. On their first full working day together, Brian played Asher several works-in-progress, including the backing tracks for "Sloop John B" (recorded as early as 12th July 1965, with the vocals eventually added in December) and a song tentatively called "In My Childhood", which was eventually to turn into "You Still Believe In Me". There was quite a lot of work to listen to, but listening together served to set the type of relationship that Brian was seeking.

Asher was aware of Brian's love of The Four Freshmen and so, during the pre-writing discussions, he asked if Brian knew about the Hi-Los*. Asher was keen on their jazz-like vocals – "polite jazz" as he called it.

Asher and Brian discussed 'standards' and other songs that featured the sort of chord changes that interested Brian, and Asher introduced him to the song "Stella By Starlight". In mid-October, Brian arranged for a session at United Recorders to cut an orchestral version of this song, together with "How Deep Is The Ocean" and a tack-on track at the end of the three-hour session called "Three Blind Mice". The exact reason for this session is a mystery, as it does not seem to relate to any likely Beach Boys' work. It is possible that Brian, with an eye to the enticing Sinatra-styled market, cut the tracks with a mainstream singer in mind. It is also possible that he wanted to move further up the orchestral learning curve before fully tackling *Pet Sounds*.

For these sessions, Brian brought back Dick Reynolds, the arranger from the Christmas LP, and used the experienced 'Bones' Howe as engineer. Of the three tracks, the one minute and fifteen seconds snippet of "Three Blind Mice" is the most typically Brian-sounding, and shows him trying out plucked strings in a repeated motif against a background of heavy drums and deep growling brass. At the end Brian is heard to say that it has been a good experiment, intimating that his purpose was exploratory rather than just

---

* The Hi-Los at that time included Clark Burroughs who would go on to be part of the nineties tribute album "A Jazz Portrait of Brian Wilson."

recording another track.

Before the writing sessions, Brian and Asher got to know each other better through wide-ranging discussions at Brian's Beverly Hills home.

The meetings were very much to Brian's late-rising timetable, which Asher quickly had to adjust to. The sessions could also be interrupted at any time by Brian's desire to watch shows like *Flipper* on TV. Tony interpreted this as an example of a lack of sophistication, as he witnessed his co-writer cry at the sad events in the storylines.

Asher remembers how they talked mainly about three things: music in many forms, from classical to pop hits; spiritualism in the form of different approaches to religion and the metaphysics of certain philosophies; and their feelings for women.

Brian's desire to move away from the cars-and-girls lyrics of "traditional" Beach Boys material was strong, but his departure would be one of perspective and maturity, rather than a complete change of subject matter. Whilst others around him in America, such as Dylan, P.F. Sloan and members of the folk rock movement were writing material that addressed the rapidly darkening world of war and political struggle, Brian wanted to evoke the bittersweetness of adolescence and describe more maturing relationship issues. The hot rods and coupes might be less prominent, but the girls were still central. There is no indication, save for the covers of songs like "The Times They Are A-Changin'" on the *Party* album, that Brian was ever interested in anything "political". Neither Vietnam nor the civil rights movement seemed to trouble Brian's radar. The bigger perspective of current affairs and world issues was arguably beyond his comprehension; certainly it was something he was isolated from. The demands of Brian's high pressure career of the previous four years had kept him in an all-encompassing work "bubble" which left room only for music and, increasingly, girls.

In the way Brian discussed women, Asher felt it was almost as if Brian wasn't yet married. When they spoke in depth of the girls they admired, Asher was on the verge of discomfort.

"Brian acknowledged specific affection for Marilyn," Asher remembers, "but at the same time he wasn't sure how guys could be focused on just one person when there were others around. He certainly had a deep affection for both Marilyn's other sisters, but as one of them [Barbara] was very young, maybe less than 14 at the time, I wasn't sure that I wanted to go down that conversational road. There was surprising candour when he spoke. It was whatever was in his head, but it was a bit embarrassing when he spoke about Diane or Barbara. We'd go to the Rovell's house sometimes, and the family were impulsive, very welcoming and they loved Brian. All in all, perhaps very unlike his own family. But …with the sisters…I mean age-wise, and they were his sisters-in-law!"

The lyrics of certain of Brian's songs at that time ("Don't Hurt My Little Sister", "The Little Girl I Once Knew" and "All Dressed Up (For School)") certainly support the possibility that Brian was experiencing emotional confusion. "All Dressed Up (For School)" is especially interesting as it was unreleased at the time, despite being a fully formed Beach Boys' song. It seems likely that the risqué nature of the lyrics that referred to attraction to a schoolgirl, and the line *"Oooh, what a turn on"* in particular, was deemed unsuitable for the group's wholesome image. (The song would eventually emerge in the nineties as a bonus track on one of the Capitol twofers, *Little Deuce Coupe/ All Summer Long*.) Asher and Brian enjoyed and discussed The Lovin' Spoonful's songs "Did You Ever Have To Make Up Your Mind?" and "Younger Girl" which dealt with similar topics of attraction to young women. It was reflective of the changes occurring in pop at the time, as writers moved away from traditional "safe" subject matter. Asher further supports these possible confusions in Brian's mind, "Marilyn was very focused on Brian, but he felt bad about not being better…for her. If we went out together to get some food or something, and we saw a pretty girl, we would talk about her and our feelings of attraction. I think that maybe Brian was emotionally a few years before his actual age…in a sort of adolescence."

In fact, this emotional immaturity may have been part of Brian's key to getting successfully inside the head of a teenager in his writing

"The things that impressed me most about Brian were, first off, his songwriting talents," says Billy Strange, a session guitarist who had worked with Brian pre-*Pet Sounds*. "He was writing things at that time that were 'right down the throats' of his listening audience. *The Teenagers*! He had an innate sense of what they wanted to hear, and would buy on record… He didn't write *down* to them, as many other writer before him, but gave them melodies and lyrics that were extremely grown-up and meaningful to them."

Brian's conversations with Tony indicate his preoccupations and state of mind, but they also served as the bedrock for the songwriting between the pair. Asher remembers discussion of feelings and break-ups leading to particular moods, which in turn led into songs. Certainly the lyrics for "You Still Believe In Me" would fit Brian's apparent feelings for Marilyn particularly closely: *"I know perfectly well I'm not where I should be/ I've been very aware you've been patient with me."*

The actual writing sessions were a synthesis of the two men's ideas. Asher recalls how they began:

"It was a bit stilted at first, but then it went swimmingly. I would adjust my time of arrival to allow for Brian's later rising, and we'd talk about things and make connections. It was not limiting for me. I was a simple young guy, having a great time. It was all fun to talk about. We'd talk then about a particular concept, not necessarily all about love and relationships. It was not conceived at the time specifically as a love/relationships album, although we did say very particularly that it would be 'a new approach to where The Beach Boys are'. We aimed to forget all that had gone before – it was not going to be 'just another Beach Boys album'. Brian wanted it to be an honest album. He thought that there was no depth to the main hits."*

The collaboration soon took on its own momentum, forming a sort of co-operative ebb and flow. Sometimes Brian would drive things forward from his musical ideas, and sometimes Asher would take the lead with lyrical ideas. Asher would also suggest musical alterations, while Brian suggested lyrics. The spirit of give and take helped the main body of writing be completed within the three-week period of Asher's leave of absence. However, progress was not always as smooth as this timeframe would imply.

"Brian was always hearing something quite different to what I was hearing," Asher recalls. "Brian had the concept in his head, but it was a successful collaboration because we would take something, change it and make it better. Brian would talk about the song to me, but I would not necessarily be hearing what he heard. He'd get very excited, but I wasn't always aware why. It was all a bit amazing!"

To reach the 'feels' for the songs, Brian tried fragments of ideas at the piano or started to develop a particular melody: form and tempo often dictated the subject matter of the lyric. Asher explains this in connection with "I Just Wasn't Made For These Times": "That's not a love song in the normal way," he says, "unless it's in some way love of self. Brian knew that he wanted it to be a song about feeling that you didn't fit into your time. I picked up on that idea straight away, and from the fragments of ideas he had I wrote a very different lyric."

Brian taped the emerging musical ideas, and Asher took them home to

---

* There are some reasonable grounds to question if at any point, Brian was subconsciously, or even overtly, considering this as a solo project. The single release of "Caroline No," on 7th March 1966, ahead of the album, trailed as a solo outing – apparently at Brian's request – suggests that this solo course was considered by Capitol, not just because the song happened to feature no other Beach Boy involvement. Its comparative poor chart showing, reaching only Number 32 as "Sloop John B" (issued on 23rd March as ongoing group product rather than as a pointer to the next album) leapfrogged above it, may well have cancelled any tentative plans for a solo project. Capitol Records, and the other members of the group, were only interested in Top Ten Beach Boys product.

work on lyrics or to add extra verses for the next day, when he and Brian edited, extended or refined them to fit the music. Attention was paid to how well certain sung words would sound set to music. For example, Asher was aware of the frequent need to use words incorporating long vowel sounds, or syllables that could be stretched as with the final *"I want to cry"* line in "You Still Believe In Me." The two men sang lines back and forth to each other to find which words sang best.

"Brian would give or suggest lines to me, but his primary role in the whole relationship was more reacting to what I brought to him rather than producing it himself," Asher explains. "Similarly, I would react to his musical ideas and suggest things if I saw fit. However, he did defer to me on many occasions, trusting my judgements with words. It was the music that was really his thing. My career had been very involved with words, which is probably why Brian saw potential in us working together. The whole thing became a successful joint editorial process. I think it's fair to say that Brian is a better counter-puncher than going off on his own."

Asher soon became aware that Brian's abilities enabled him to develop sub-melodies underneath the main lines. "Brian played the bass line with his left hand – the feel of the song, or the 'attitude' to put it another way – while he developed the rest with his right," Asher remembers. "His chord and key changes were often surprising."

Despite Brian's lead role in the musical development, Tony did have musical input on "Caroline No", "I Just Wasn't Made For These Times" and "That's Not Me".

As they continued working together, Brian allowed himself to develop a conscious romanticism similar to the love trilogy on *Today*. The song "Don't Talk (Put Your Head On My Shoulder)" demonstrates this perfectly,

*"I can hear so much in your sighs*
*And I can see so much in your eyes*
*These are words we both could say*
*But don't talk, put your head on my shoulder."*

This romanticism extends to "God Only Knows," which, unbelievably, was completely written within half an hour by Asher and Brian. Starting with the confession, *"I may not always love you,"* it goes on to surrender to the bond of love, *"God only knows what I'd be without you".*

"I think it was his feminine side emerging," says Asher. "He had his high voice, which could be seen as youthful or feminine, but at the same time he wanted to be deeper in both senses and more mature. I think that *Pet Sounds* took him through his own adolescence. He had lost out on maturity time by being in the band. He had other people to do things for him. Even today, he might not know how to deposit a cheque. His development had been somewhat stunted in certain areas."

Certainly Brian seemed confident and happy during the writing of the album. Once the quickly recorded demos showed that the collaboration was working, the atmosphere mellowed and there was a lot of laughing and joking.

"Boy, I wanted to do something different, and this sure is different!" Brian told Asher with a smile. "Boy the guys will be surprised! Hey, people are going to realise that this isn't a Brian Wilson lyric."

At the same time, Brian was aware that people might not like the new direction.

"Uh Oh … Mike's gonna be *real* surprised…" he conceded to his partner.

Brian and Tony were writing without any reference to, or input from, the other band members. Brian was not being paranoid. The mood and subject matter was sufficiently removed from the light-hearted hedonism at the heart of much of the band's previous material. Brian was taking the introspection of "In My Room" a whole lot further.

While previous lyrics dealt with absolutes expressed clearly in the present tense, suddenly the conditional was creeping in. The recurrence of "could" and "would" emphasised the fragility and tentative nature of Brian's relationships in songs like "Here Today" and "I Just Wasn't Made For These Times."

Other themes unlikely to be welcomed by Mike Love included the pre-sexual yearning of "Wouldn't It Be Nice" and the passing of innocence in "Caroline No".

The individual songs contain some limited input from other writers. "I Know There's An Answer," with original writing credits to Brian Wilson and Terry Sachen (a Beach Boys road manager in the mid sixties) predates Asher's involvement. The song was originally called "Hang On To Your Ego," a title Mike Love dismissed as unsuitable. The more specific root of Mike's worries may well have been the fact that, at that period of time, descriptions of the effects of LSD included alterations of the user's ego. It is very likely that by this time, as Brian moved into a different Hollywood-based group of friends, he would have been exposed to LSD. Mike's later additional credit on the song dated from this intervention, when he presumably suggested lyric changes to move the song away from drug inferences.

Mike Love's writing credit on "Wouldn't It Be Nice," gained retrospectively during an early nineties court case, is less easy to explain. When Tony Asher was asked in a 1997 interview to describe the extent of

Mike's involvement, he replied "None, whatsoever." The song was written while Mike and the rest of the Beach Boys – bar Brian – were on tour, and Asher dismisses the claims made by Mike's lawyers that he influenced the writing during a phone call. Tony suspects that the subsequent credit may perhaps arise from some vocal changes and suggestions that Mike may have made during the recording of the song.

Another more famous song to emerge from the *Pet Sounds* writing and recording sessions was "Good Vibrations." It was held back from the album because Brian wanted to continue experimenting with the arrangement. Asher's original lyrics to the classic tune described the magic moment in nascent romance,

*"She's already working on my brain,*
*I only looked in her eyes,*
*But I picked up something I can't explain,*
*Good, good, good vibrations yeah*

*I bet I know what she's like,*
*And I feel how right she'd be for me,*
*It's when, how she comes on so strong,*
*And I wonder what she's picking up from me,*
*I hope it's good, good, good vibrations."*

Brian recorded a track for the song on 18th February, adding his lead vocal using these words. The celebratory nature of the words certainly made it possible to include the song on the album, and indeed the title did appear on a list of tracks for the album that Brian submitted to Capitol around late February 1966. Interestingly, this list also included "Sloop John B" ahead of its single release date, which suggests Brian was happier about *its* inclusion on the album than has often been supposed. However, Brian wasn't satisfied with "Good Vibrations" and held it back. Subsequent sessions held both before and after the release of *Pet Sounds*, saw Mike Love write a new set of words and change the chorus to "*I'm picking up good vibrations.*" In the light of recent composition credit revisions, some people may argue that there is a case for Asher's name appearing as co-writer.

Mike Love later laid some of the blame for his lack of writing credits on his uncle Murry, who was managing the publishing business at this time. Asher also had to deal with Murry in formalising the business aspects of his writing partnership with Brian, and by his account Murry wasn't very generous. Tony settled for a rather miserly quarter per cent royalty. Though Asher eventually received payments estimated at around $60,000 and still receives additional royalties, the amounts represent a comparatively small payment considering the sales and status of the songs.

Asher recalls that Murry was not particularly pleasant to deal with, and that he could see some of the pressure that Brian was under from within the family. In Asher's opinion, Murry's oppressive nature was a major part of Brian's emotional problems.

At Brian's invitation, Asher attended some of the instrumental and vocal sessions, but most of his time after the sabbatical was taken up by his advertising job. Contact with the rest of the Beach Boys on their return from touring was minimal but cordial. Today, he looks back at his involvement on *Pet Sounds* with pride and happiness.

"I hope everyone will understand how deeply appreciative I am of the praise for my work. It is very gratifying and I accept it only with genuine humility. I know how fortunate I was (and am) to be working with Brian. He is just the sort of catalyst that raises one's work to its highest level. I mean that sincerely."

Whilst other writers contributed in a comparatively small way, it is without doubt the lyrics that emerged from the very personal discussions between Brian and Tony that are one of the keys to the album's lasting beauty and superiority.

With his collaborator's work completed, Brian turned to the new reality of fully constructing and realising the instrumental tracks that he was devoloping in his head.

# Chapter 4
# "HEY CHUCK, COULD WE BRING A HORSE IN HERE?"*:
# RECORDING THE CONCEPT.
## Part I: The Instrumental Tracks

*Typical Western equipment.*

*"The sessions for* Pet Sounds *were especially entertaining. [They] weren't exactly free-form, because there was an organisational concept, but there was a lot of room for surprises…Brian was a thinker, a creator."*

– Hal Blaine (*Pet Sounds* drummer)

*"Whereas The Beatles were taking discrete elements from other musical genres and grafting them onto pop, Brian moulded a sound that extended the vocabulary of pop in its own right. Familiar musical instruments used in peculiar combinations are transmogrified into something else: new sonorities."*

– Peter Lacey (Singer/songwriter of Beam,
Paul Williams' favourite "child of Brian" album)

---

* This quote is from Brian in the studio, talking to Chuck Britz during the "Hang On To Your Ego" sessions. Chuck replied, "I beg your pardon." No horse participation in Brian Wilson recording sessions was ever noted.

Having had some home time, both writing with Tony Asher and enjoying the Thanksgiving/Christmas season, Brian began to immerse himself in recording – secure in a "bubble" away from the turmoil of the changing wider world. However, if politics didn't interest Brian, he was certainly aware of what was happening in the wider musical world, as his comments to a reporter from *KRLA Beat* illustrate.

"I think the British influence in American production has been stimulating because a lot of the creative producers were eclipsed, and a lot of their artistic records lost their significance," Brian told the journalist. "I think they tried that much harder to make a unique sounding record that stuck out. For that reason alone, I think the British influence – in the end – produced a good result. I think the Beatles' influence is so far-reaching that it's hard to say what their influence is to date. I think it will show up even in the next five years... Bob Dylan stands for such a large segment of the folk industry. He stands for the contemporary and liberated minds – I think – of today, and so many people are considered 'Dylan people', but there are (also) 'Byrd people' and 'Stone people'. I think it's all really part of a movement of liberation – of self-liberating feeling. And I think he's definitely the king – by his talents alone. The protest records are very direct – outside of Dylan – I think that Dylan is very implicit, and his lyrics have to be read into for a long time. I think in that protest bag, most of the protest songs are very direct, and they can only mean one thing."

As with virtually any part of The Beach Boys' sixties history, there was in 1966 a constant state of overlap between releases, writing and recording. For instance, "Sloop John B" from *Pet Sounds*, was released as a single on 23rd March 1966 – ten months after it was recorded. Gaps and overlaps were often caused by Brian being forced to fit recording session with the Beach Boys around the touring group's other commitments. This was one of the reasons why Brian was spending more time working with experienced studio session players, though his motivation was not just logistical. Brian was becoming ever more keen to produce instrumental textures beyond his group's capabilities.

Freed from the restrictions of touring, Brian was able to work almost constantly during the period – so long as he could rely on musicians outside the Beach Boys. Even during his short period of intense writing with Asher in the Autumn of 1965, he was already working on recording some tracks and ideas for what would become *Pet Sounds*. Brian played works-in-progress of a number of tracks to his co-writing partner, including "Sloop John B", and "You Still Believe In Me" (aka "In My Childhood") which, according to the session contract sheet, wasn't recorded until 24th January 1966. Tony clearly remembers working with an existing track that featured a bicycle bell that could not be removed. "Wouldn't It Be Nice" is dated at two days before on the 22nd January. It is reasonable to assume that certain details on the sheet for 24th January are wrong, possibly just the song title or perhaps more likely that this was the date when the song's introduction was re-worked.

Tony certainly recalls helping out with the sound on the early version of "You Still Believe In Me".

"I plucked the [piano] strings with paper clips, hairpins, bobbi pins and several other things until Brian got the sound he wanted," Tony recalls. "This [intro] section, by the way, was recorded separately after the track had been cut and then spliced onto the track."

It is important to understand that while Brian was aware that he was pushing new boundaries with his music and building up to making a truly great album, during this period he wasn't always consciously working on separate bodies of work. Whilst his co-operation with Tony Asher was a discrete project, the use that Brian was to put the songs to was probably less formed in his mind, aside from the fact that he had to deliver an LP.

It is very likely that, whilst Capitol were releasing *Summer Days (And Summer Nights!!)* and *Beach Boys Party*, Brian had already been leading tracking sessions with larger groups of session musicians in the autumn of 1965. There is no dispute that the session for the title track "Pet Sounds", known originally as "Run, James, Run", was held on November 17th 1965. A couple of weeks before this, on 1st November, Brian had recorded the music known as "Trombone Dixie" which has subsequently been linked to *Pet Sounds* by its inclusion on CD re-issues since the early nineties.

After Brian had recorded tracks for "Sloop John B" – which was not originally conceived as part of the *Pet Sounds* project – the previous July and album title track the previous November, the majority of the music tracks for the actual *Pet Sounds* songs were recorded between mid-January and mid-March 1966. Brian used a collection of top LA session musicians built around the nucleus of Spector regulars Jay Migliori (sax and clarinet), Steve Douglas (sax and other instruments), Carol Kaye (bass) and Hal Blaine (drums and percussion).* Large numbers of musicians did not come cheap and were available only to Brian because Capitol's A&R executive Karl Engemann realised the prudence of investing in Brian's talent. When *Pet Sounds* was funded to give Brian free rein over his choice of players, it was as if the garret painter had suddenly been given pristine canvasses and fine new brushes, allowing ideas to flow with uninterrupted vigour.

The group vocal tracks were mostly cut during March and the first half of

* For a full list of musicians, see appendix

April, though Brian recorded some of his own vocals alone during the instrumental recording sessions, as he tried his own voice as leads and backgrounds for the songs. These sessions would usually have taken place within a day or two of the backing track being recorded, according to engineer Chuck Britz.

Britz was instrumental in Brian choosing to record the majority of *Pet Sounds* at Western. Brian was by now experienced with a number of the local studios. He appreciated RCA and Sunset Sound, as well as the obvious draw of recording at Gold Star where the mighty Phil Spector chose to work. Brian certainly preferred Western for the vocals that his group specialised in, liking the echo chamber for its "balanced and fat" sound. However, with Brian working more and more with larger groups of session players, it was essential to work in a studio that could accommodate them physically. Brian had seen Phil Spector work with large groups of musicians, often doubling or tripling instruments to achieve his huge trademark wall of sound. When Brian had first assembled a large group of musicians – many of whom were Spector regulars – to record the instrumental track for "California Girls", he wasn't convinced that Western was large enough to accommodate such a big band and recorded instead at Columbia, then home to the only eight-track in town. Brian brought the backing track to Western to overdub some vocals. Britz persuaded Brian to give Western a chance for a couple of *Pet Sounds* tracks.

"Once we started we did all of them," Britz reflected with vindication. Though the engineer was not completely factually correct. The unravelling of which *Pet Sounds* track was recorded in which studio has always been a tortuous task, clouded by the fact that sessions were seldom single-once-and-for-all occasions at this stage. Brian might record a basic track at one studio on one day, overdub somewhere else the next, and later finish with vocals at a third. Certainly it is true to say that about half of *Pet Sounds* was fully recorded at Western, but as the appendices note, Gold Star and Sunset Sound were also used. Brian is quoted as liking Western's vocal sound, but many of the vocal tracks were recorded at least in part at Columbia's studio, the tracks concerned being "Wouldn't It Be Nice", "I'm Waiting For The Day", "God Only Knows", "Here Today" and "I Just Wasn't Made For These Times". The attraction of using Columbia for these particular five tracks was the eight-track board that allowed Brian more vocal possibilities. Even then though, tracks may well have been brought back to Western later for overdubbing or changing. The whole exact story of which bits of which tracks were recorded where is never likely to be fully available.

Barney Kessel's son David, a great fan of both Spector and Brian, was taken to sessions at both Gold Star and Western as a youngster before

*A Columbia Studios acetate.*

growing up to work at both. He explains the essential differences between the two studios:

"Gold Star's Studio A, where all the classic cuts were made, was acoustically great with an incredible echo chamber. Stan Ross and Dave Gold customised the board, and tailored the rooms to really suit Rock 'n' Roll and Pop. They knew how to blend and capture the essence of instruments... The several studios at Western, at one point they had three studios going, had different acoustics. They were set up more for *general* recording and catered for a broader range. It was a Hollywood studio with different clients like Sinatra. They had a professional sound, but it was cleaner and maybe more nondescript. Brian may well have worked in more than one room there, because if one room was booked you would simply move into another."

There is still discussion as to which of the Western studios was usually used for *Pet Sounds*, and I have indeed heard conflicting accounts from two of the most prominent session players. However, judging by size, photographic evidence, and Chuck Britz's discussion with writer Andrew Doe in Western 3 in the mid-eighties, it is reasonably certain that the main studio used was indeed No 3. That is not to say that Brian may not have used No 2 on occasion, and it is believed to have been used during the *Beach Boys' Party* sessions shortly before.

Still, for Brian most of the ambience of a session came from the working with the players and translation of his ideas, rather than the studio itself. He would take special care to mike the musicians to take account of different groupings of players. Brian's friend Danny Hutton, later of Three Dog Night, attended some of the *Pet Sounds* sessions and was impressed by Brian's ability to get big and rich sounds in each studio with what appeared

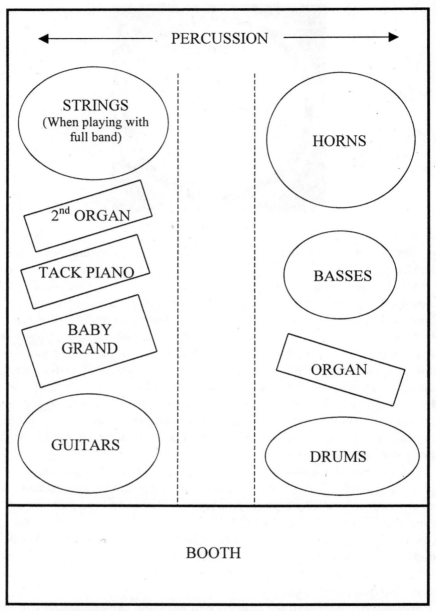

*A standard* Pet Sounds *set-up at Western reconstructed with the help of Hal Blaine. Measurements 15 ft. x 23 ft. approx.*

to be casual placing of the mikes. Danny saw it as an innate ability to know how the different levels of sound would blend together.

Whilst Brian and Phil Spector were certainly the hottest producers around at the time, there was a critical difference between them. Spector had Jack Nitzsche as his in-house arranger to construct his grandiose ideas from individual musical building blocks. Spector certainly had musical ability, but was not himself an especially talented musician. What made Brian so extraordinary was that he needed little outside help at all. He was a wonderful singer, had mastery, or at least extreme competence, over several instruments, and most importantly he had the ability to translate the arrangements he heard in his head into actual music. For all their immense talent, The Beatles were extremely reliant on producer George Martin in translating their ideas and ambitions into musical reality. Brian Wilson had the abilities of singer, player, arranger and producer combined; none of his competitors on either side of the Atlantic could come close. With all these talents, he was able to draw on his quickly-learnt studio knowledge to begin work on his biggest and most intricate project to date.

The atmosphere of the *Pet Sounds* recordings was important. The musicians were vastly experienced players mostly in their thirties and early forties. They had seen many young hotshot producers before. However, it did not take too long before they realised something special was taking place. Diane Rovell, Brian's sister-in-law, was employed by this time as a pre-session organiser in the role of contractor, after having been trained for the post by drummer Hal Blaine. Diane remembered the sessions, "The musicians were great. There were times they would go, 'Hey, it's not the money that's important, it's the opportunity to work with Brian.' Everybody was having fun…the people we worked with in the studio were incredible."

© Capitol Photo Archives

*Brian directs.*

CAPITOL RECORDS
(Employer's name)
0402

**Phonograph Recording Contract Blank**

# AMERICAN FEDERATION OF MUSICIANS 105852
## OF THE UNITED STATES AND CANADA

Local Union No. 47

THIS CONTRACT for the personal services of musicians, made this **11th** day of **February**, 19**66** between the undersigned employer (hereinafter called the "employer") and **eight** musicians (hereinafter called "employees"). *(including the leader)*

WITNESSETH, That the employer hires the employees as musicians severally on the terms and conditions below, and as further specified on reverse side. The leader represents that the employees already designated have agreed to be bound by said terms and conditions. Each employee yet to be chosen shall be so bound by said terms and conditions upon agreeing to accept his employment. Each employee may enforce this agreement. The employees severally agree to render collectively to the employer services as musicians in the orchestra under the leadership of **Steven Douglas Kreisman** as follows:

Name and Address of Place of Engagement **Western Recorders, 6000 Sunset Blvd., Hollywood, Calif.**

Date(s) and Hours of Employment **2-11-66    9:00 AM – 12:00 Noon**
**12:30 Noon – 12:30 PM**

Type of Engagement: Recording for phonograph records only

Plus pension contributions as specified on reverse side hereof.

WAGE AGREED UPON $ **Union scale (including overtime & tracking)** *(Terms and amount)*

This wage includes expenses agreed to be reimbursed by the employer in accordance with the attached schedule, or a schedule to be furnished the employer on or before the date of engagement.

To be paid _____ *(Specify when payments are to be made)*

Upon request by the American Federation of Musicians and Canada (herein called the "Federation") or the local in whose jurisdiction the employees shall perform hereunder, the employer either shall make advance payment hereunder or shall post an appropriate bond.

| | |
|---|---|
| Employer's name and **Capitol Records, Inc.** | Leader's name **Steven D. Kreisman**   Local No. **47** |
| authorized signature | Leader's signature |
| Street address **1750 North Vine Street** | Street address **6950 Chisholm Avenue** |
| **Hollywood 28, Calif. Ho. 2-6252** | **Van Nuys, California** |
| City   State   Phone | City   State |

(1) Label name **Capitol**

Session no. _____

| Master no. | No. of minutes | TITLES OF TUNES | Master no. | No. of minutes | TITLES OF TUNES |
|---|---|---|---|---|---|
| | | Don't Talk | | | |
| | | (track) | | | |

| (2) Employee's name (As on Social Security card) Last First Initial | (3) Home address (Give street, city and state) | (4) Local Union no. | (5) Social Security number | (6) Scale wages | (7) Pension contribution |
|---|---|---|---|---|---|
| (Leader) | 6950 Chisholm Avenue | | | | |
| Kreisman, Steven D. | Van Nuys, California | 47 | | $203.36 | 16.28 |
| Brita, Charles D. (Contr.) | 4502 Wawona St. Los Angeles 65, Calif. | 47 | | 203.36 | 16.28 |
| Capp, Frank | 3017 Dona Bonita Studio City, Calif. | 47 | | 113.88 | 9.11 |
| Campbell, Glen | 8502 Allenwood Road Los Angeles 46, Calif. | 47 | | 101.68 | 8.14 |
| Strange, William E. | 17312 Osborne St. Northridge, Calif. | 47 | | 101.68 | 8.14 |
| Kaye, Carol | 4905 Forman North Hollywood, Calif. | 47 | | 101.68 | 8.14 |
| Pitz, Lyle | 1971 No. Curson Avenue Los Angeles 46, Calif. | 47 | | 101.68 | 8.14 |
| de Lory, Alfred V. | 5524 Ruthwood Drive Calabasas, California | 47 | | 101.68 | 8.14 |
| Blaine, Hal | 2441 Castilian Drive Hollywood 28, Calif. | 47 | | 101.68 | 8.14 |

CONTRACT RECEIVED
FEB 1966
WARD ARCHER
PRESIDENT

(8) Total Pension Contributions (Sum of Column (7)) $ _____
Make check payable in this amount to "AFM & EPW Fund"

FOR FUND USE ONLY:
Date pay't rec'd _____ Amt. paid _____ Date posted _____ By _____
Form B-4 Rev. 4-59

*One of the* Pet Sounds *contract session sheets – this one with Steve Douglas (Kreisman) as contractor.*

*Carol Kaye.*

Hal Blaine had taken the contractor role for some time, most importantly being the person who booked the session players. His role was also central during Brian's sessions, because he was the in-house organiser as players assembled, and an essential centre of the humorous banter that went on. An initially sceptical veteran of sessions with the likes of Count Basie and Sinatra, Blaine gradually became more appreciative of Brian's talents.

"I watched him grow," Blaine says. "I saw that he wasn't just a punk kid. I could hear that his finished products were wonderful... I always wanted to hear the song...whether it was on the piano, or hummed...or sung as a few words...to get the basic feel. Brian would have chord charts, but not like main arrangers who'd have more than just the basic map. Some composers could and would really write music. But Brian would have most of it in his head."

"Brian *always* brought written out charts for most of the musicians..." Fender bass player Carol Kaye recalls. "He wrote the charts himself, you could tell from the illegibility of them sometimes. The notes were sometimes on the wrong side of the stems etc. He didn't hire a professional copyist like the rest of the arrangers did."

Charts aside, the basic "*feel*" referred to by Blaine was crucial to the sessions.

Phonograph Recording Contract Blank

# AMERICAN FEDERATION OF MUSICIANS
## OF THE UNITED STATES AND CANADA

(CAPITOL RECORDS)
(Employer's name)
0807

Nº 247425

Local Union No.

THIS CONTRACT for the personal services of musicians, made this 10 day of MARCH 19 66 between the undersigned employer (hereinafter called the "employer" and WESTERN musicians (including the leader) (hereinafter called "employees").

WITNESSETH, That the employer hires the employees as musicians severally on the terms and conditions below, and as further specified on reverse side. The leader represents that the employees already designated have agreed to be bound by said terms and conditions. Each employee yet to be chosen shall be so bound by said terms and conditions upon agreeing to accept his employment. Each employee may enforce this agreement. The employees severally agree to render collectively to the employer services as musicians in the orchestra under the leadership of

HAL BLAINE

Name and Address of Place of Engagement WESTERN RECORDERS (BEACH BOYS)

Date(s) and Hours of Employment MARCH 10, 1966   12:30 AM to 4:15 AM

Type of Engagement: Recording for phonograph records only UNION SCALE Plus pension contributions as WAGE AGREED UPON (TRACK) (time and amount) specified on reverse side hereof.

This wage includes expenses agreed to be reimbursed by the employer in accordance with the attached schedule, or a schedule to be furnished the employer on or before the date of engagement.

To be paid WITHIN 15 DAYS (Specify when payments are to be made)

Upon request by the American Federation of Musicians of the United States and Canada (herein called the "Federation") or the local in whose jurisdiction the employees shall perform hereunder the employer either shall make advance payment hereunder or shall post an appropriate bond.

| | | |
|---|---|---|
| Employer's name and | CAPITOL RECORDS | Leader's name HAL BLAINE Local No. 47 |
| authorized signature | | Leader's signature Jay Migliori |
| Street address | 1750 N VINE | Street address 2441 CASTILLIAN |
| Hollywood CALIF HO2.6252 | | HOLLYWOOD 28 CALIF |
| City State Phone | | City State |

(1) Label Name Capitol

CONTRACT RECEIVED MAR 28 1966

| No. of | | | No. of | |
|---|---|---|---|---|
| Master No. Minutes | TITLES OF TUNES | Master No. | Minutes | TITLES OF TUNES |
| | | | 2:30 | GOD ONLY KNOWS |

WARD ARCHER ASST TO PRESIDENT

| (2) Employee's Name (As on Social Security Card) Last First Initial | (3) Home Address (Give Street, City and State) | (4) Local Union No. | (5) Social Security Number | (6) Scale Wages | (7) Pension Contribution |
|---|---|---|---|---|---|
| | 2441 CASTILLIAN Hollywood 28 CALIF | | | | |
| BLAINE, HAL | 1701 N. LINCOLN | 47 | | | |
| MIGLIORI, JAY | Panorama CALIF. | 47 | | | |
| HARTMAN, LEONARD | BEVERLY HILLS CALIF | 47 | | | |
| POHLMAN, M.B. | 617 ROCKCLIFF DR L.A. CALIF | 47 | | | |
| RITZ, LYLE | 1971 N GLASON AVE L.A. CALIF | 47 | | | |
| FORTINA, CARL L | 238 NO. ORANGE DR Hollywood 36 CALIF | 47 | | | |
| MAROCCO, FRANK | 7067 WHITAKER AVE VAN NUYS CALIF | 47 | | | |
| MALARSKY, LEONARD | 3801 DOS PALOS DR L.A. 28 CALIF | 47 | | | |
| SHARP SIDNEY | 1000 N. LA JOLLA L.A. 46 CALIF | 47 | | | |
| TERWILLIGER DARREL | 12631 ADDISON ST. NORTH HOLLYWOOD CALIF | 47 | | | |
| EHRLICH JESSE | 6960 WHITAKER AVE VAN NUYS CALIF | 47 | | | |
| KNECHTEL LAWRENCE W | VAN NOORD AVE SHERMAN OAKS, CALIF | 47 | | | |
| KAYE CAROL | 4905 FORMAN NO. HOLLYWOOD CALIF | 47 | | | |
| GREEN WILLIAM EARNEST | 4526 DON MIGUEL DR L.A. 8 CALIF | 47 | | 18708 | |
| BRITZ CHARLES D. | 4501 WANONA ST L.A. 65 CALIF | 47 | | | |

(8) Total Pension Contributions (Sum of Column (7)) $ Make check payable in this amount to "AFM & EPW Fund."

FOR FUND USE ONLY:
PAID APR 1 1966
Date pay't rec'd    Amt. paid    Data posted    By

Changes in W.A.    Form B-4 Rev. 4-59

"A feel was whether or not it *felt* good," Blaine explains gnomically. "People still danced in those days, so the rhythm and tempo of a record was very important. It was the pulse. Brian would come to me sometimes and we'd listen to a playback, to see if it felt right. Sometimes there might be little odd mistakes here and there, but if the feel was right we might go with it."

"As for getting the feel, Brian was just one of those timekeepers in his head," says Sax player Jim Horn. "He really had the rhythm in his brain and knew how he wanted it to feel. We didn't have click tracks; you had to lock right into the pocket. He made sure everyone felt that with him."

When listening to the various tracking sessions now available commercially, one of the most frequent refrains is Brian urging the musicians to "keep it real tight," while emphasising particular rhythms by banging on the console. These percussive *feels* are one of the most obvious and progressive aspects of the record. Accents, variations of tempo, and the comparative density of the percussion are all of prime importance to the whole, and Brian is often heard striving to align the drums and percussion closer to what he can hear in his head.

"He knew where he wanted to go, but at times no-one else knew," says pianist Don Randi. "Sometimes we would need translation of the sound and direction. We might work on the same eight bars for hours, and with the different sound combinations...well, some worked and some didn't work so well. However, some of our mistakes turned out even better than the original plan or direction. Brian was a good 'executive'; he was very smart. If he knew what he had in mind was the right thing to do, he'd do it with us until we got it right."

"As a musician, he was able to sit at a piano, or behind a guitar, and show you," says guitarist Billy Strange, who had worked with Brian before *Pet Sounds*, "not just to sort of explain, but to demonstrate the feel and emotion of what he wished you to play. It was always very plain and concise."

Before the days of multi-tracking, drop-ins and layered overdubbing, the most crucial tools in recording were the live musicians, so the time Brian spent with them before the recording started was of prime importance. All the players would be called for the beginning of the session, even if they were not required until near its end. Sessions were usually set for three hours, perhaps with a half or full hour of overtime. If it looked like it would be a long date, the session would be altered to what was known as a double-date. This would be two three-hour sessions with an hour in between – less expensive than going an hour or more overtime. Payments came from The Beach Boys 'pot' at Capitol Records, which was by this time handsomely in credit. So at the time, Brian didn't have huge financial constraints.

Indeed, Hal Blaine recalls an occasion when an accountant came to a

Capitol Records
(Employer's name)

**Phonograph Recording Contract Blank**

# AMERICAN FEDERATION OF MUSICIANS

0416

OF THE UNITED STATES AND CANADA

105856

Local Union No. 47

THIS CONTRACT for the personal services of musicians, made this **14th** day of **February**, 19**66** between the undersigned employer (hereinafter called the "employer") and **Fifteen** musicians (hereinafter called "employees")

(Including the leader)

WITNESSETH, That the employer hires the employees as musicians severally on the terms and conditions below, and as further specified on reverse side. The leader represents that the employees already designated have agreed to be bound by said terms and conditions. Each employee yet to be chosen shall be so bound by said terms and conditions upon agreeing to accept his employment. Each employee may enforce this agreement. The employees severally agree to render collectively to the employer services as musicians in the orchestra under the leadership of **Steven Douglas Kreisman** as follows:

Name and Address of Place of Engagement **Gold Star Recorders, 6252 Santa Monica Blvd, Hollywood, California**

Date(s) and Hours of Employment **2-14-66 7:30 PM to 10:30 PM**
**10:30 PM to 11:30 PM**

Type of Engagement: Recording for phonograph records

WAGE AGREED UPON $ **Union scale (including overtime & tracking)** Plus pension contributions as specified on reverse side hereof.

(Terms and amount)

This wage includes expenses agreed to be reimbursed by the employer in accordance with the attached schedule, or a schedule to be furnished the employer on or before the date of engagement.

To be paid _____

(Specify when payments are to be made)

Upon request of the American Federation of Musicians of the United States and Canada (herein called the "Federation") or the local in whose jurisdiction the employees shall perform hereunder the employer either shall make advance payment hereunder or shall post an appropriate bond.

| Employer's name and | Capitol Records, Inc. | Leader's name | Steven D. Kreisman | Local No. 47 |
| authorized signature | | Leader's signature | | |
| Street address | 1750 No. Vine St. | Street address | 6950 Chisholm Avenue | |
| City | Hollywood 28, California | State | Van Nuys, Calif. | |
| | Ho. 2-6252 Phone | City | | State |

(1) Label name **Capitol**     Session no. _____

| Master no. | No. of minutes | TITLES OF TUNES | Master no. | No. of minutes | TITLES OF TUNES |
|---|---|---|---|---|---|
| | | I Just Wasn't Made For These (track) Things | | | |

| (2) Employee's name (As on Social Security card) Last First Initial | (3) Home address (Give street city and state) | (4) Local Union no. | (5) Social Security number | (6) Scale wages | (7) Pension contribution |
|---|---|---|---|---|---|
| (Leader) | 6950 Chisholm Avenue | | | | |
| Kreisman, Steven D. | Van Nuys, Calif. | 47 | | $244.00 | $19.54 |
| Rovell, Diane Joy | 616 No. Sierra Bonita Los Angeles, Calif. | will join | | 244.00 | 19.54 |
| Blaine, Hal | 2441 Castilian Drive Hollywood 28, Calif. | 47 | | 147.44 | 11.80 |
| Gaip, Frank | 3017 Dona Nenita Pl. Studio City, Calif. | 47 | | 137.27 | 10.98 |
| Pohlman, M.R. | 6171 Rockcliff Drive Los Angeles 28, Calif. | 47 | | 122.00 | 9.77 |
| Klein, Robert H. | 5854 Tujunga #2 North Hollywood, Calif. | 47 | | 122.00 | 9.77 |
| Migliori, Jay | 1701 No. Lincoln Burbank, Calif. | 47 | | 122.00 | 9.77 |
| Tanner, Paul O.W. | 12426 La Maida North Hollywood, Calif. | 47 | | 122.00 | 9.77 |
| Johnson, Plas | 1420 W. 59th Street Los Angeles, Calif. 90043 | 47 | | 122.00 | 9.77 |
| Berghofer, Charles | 6054 Babcock No. Hollywood, Calif. | 47 | | 122.00 | 9.77 |
| Campbell, Glen | 8502 Allenwood Los Angeles, California | 47 | | 122.00 | 9.77 |
| Morgan, Tommy | 7111 Kilty Avenue Canoga Park, Calif. | 47 | | 122.00 | 9.77 |
| Melvoin, Michael | 5445 Corteen Place No. Hollywood, Calif. | 47 | | 122.00 | 9.77 |
| Randi, Don | 2206 Nichols Cyn. Los Angeles 46, Calif. | 47 | | 122.00 | 9.77 |
| Kessel, Barney | 1727 Las Lunas Drive Glendale, Calif. | 47 | | 122.00 | 9.77 |
| Levine, Lawrence | 19811 Itasca St. Chatsworth, Calif. | will join | | 122.00 | 9.77 |

(8) Total Pension Contributions (Sum of Column (7)) $ _____

Make check payable in this amount to "AFM & EPW Fund"

FOR FUND USE ONLY:

Date pay't rec'd _____ Amt. paid _____ Date posted _____ By _____

Form B-4 Rev. 4-59

*It is possible that there was a follow on sheet to this one.*
*NB Diane Rovell as co-contractor.*

session to try to persuade Brian into moving some money out of the Sea Of Tunes account (the Beach Boys publishing company set up by Murry) as there was too much in it. Brian showed no interest in his finances, and ended up signing a big cheque just to get rid of the intrusion. "I never saw so many zeros!" grins Blaine, who goes on to explain his musical approach to Brian's sessions:

"I usually produced my own drum part, and it was used as the base to build from. There was a difference between working for Phil Spector and working for Brian. With Brian it was a smaller band so I tuned my snare lower for a bigger, fatter sound. With Phil it was a bigger band, so I had a higher snare designed to cut through the rest. Brian had *most* of what he wanted in his head, but there was always some room for us to put in pops and clicks and dings! Percussive elements came from *both* of us, often in the form of 'What can we put with that'. We would all experiment, but if he liked something he would say 'Keep that handy'. Whilst I say that I produced my own parts, which all the musicians did in some way, if it was on a ten basis I'd say it was a case of Hal – 1, Brian – 9."

The pops, clicks and dings referred to the well-known 'box of tricks' Blaine carried around with him. Although he had a drum kit pre-set at the big studios most of the time, Blaine rarely left home without his percussive kit, which contained a wide selection of rare and improvised instruments. From Blaine's inventiveness came the famed vending machine orange bottles heard on "Caroline No" that he had taped together in different cut-down sizes. Other percussion players on the *Pet Sounds* sessions, Frank Capp and Julius Wechter, point to Blaine's role as pivotal, recalling he regularly found ways to keep the musicians fresh through many takes. As well as the standard full drum kit and timpani, the album uses bells, glockenspiel, vibraphone, marimba, chimes, finger cymbals, shakers, blocks, plastic bottles and tambourine. Brian was aware of the use that Phil Spector made of percussion fills in tracks, but he used percussion to counterpoint other aspects of the track, adding extra subtle depth and colour.

To construct the desired dynamics between the players, Brian spent time with each one discussing exactly what he wanted from them. Steve Douglas acted as a filter in disseminating the horn parts to the other players who then worked their parts out as one unit to be added towards the end. Brian usually built from the rhythmic feel of the song, with Hal and the bass players.

"He'd work with the entire tune," Bassist Carol Kaye explains, "and would have individual instruments play to get a sound-balance he wanted on that instrument. We always played together on the song. He'd sometimes change the arrangement according to what he wanted. By the way, I never even knew Brian was a bass player until later. I always thought he was a

*An interesting session sheet, showing a full group of musicians seemingly working on the* Pet Sounds *instrumental track (originally recorded fully back in November). This was actually the tracking session for "Here Today".*

*Capitol Photo Archives*

*Brian working at Western with Chuck Britz (seated) and Winston Wong, the tape op. (behind).*

singer and pianist, but he sure knew how to write symphonically for bass."

"Much has been said about Brian's bass lines," says British musician and long time Brian admirer, Chris White, "... usually associated with the root note of the chord (number one of our triad) or 'walking' up and down the scale. On *Pet Sounds* this instrument is frequently given its own melody, which blends with the main tune without detracting from the plot. Nearly every track has two basses, usually acoustic and Fender with the acoustic providing the foundation and the electric doing a thing of its own – a good example being 'I Just Wasn't Made For These Times'. Another track with a great bass line is 'Sloop John B'. It is melodic and expressive but seems to avoid the root note at all costs! The same goes for 'God Only Knows' and 'Let's Go Away For Awhile' where the bass guitar plays the same note for three successive chords, none of which are the root!"

"We'd get the style and attitude of the tune after the necessary instrument balances were made, and run down his music while [Brian], still very super-composed, messed around in the booth," bassist Carol Kaye continues. "He'd give out directions for some rhythmic styles maybe to the guitars, maybe change the bass parts, back and forth as we ran down the tune. After a while we'd do a take. You have to understand, not every time would the studio musicians go into the booth to listen to the music, but we *all* went into the booth to see what Brian would be doing with *his* music. Even the great Barney Kessel (himself a subtle kidder like Brian), after listening to Brian's recording of his a cappella multi-voice overdubs, said something like 'Brian, I take back everything I ever thought about you!'…Brian acknowledged that with a slight smile, knowing that this little joke of Barney's was a high compliment! If he was trying to impress us all, he was doing a great job of it."

Whilst Brian may have usually started to build the tracks rhythmically, he didn't actually write around the drums and bass. He had each instrument's part roughly written down before the session began. Drums and percussion were often dominant, but they were part of a pre-planned whole that remained true to Brian's central notion for the song's feel. In contrast to Phil Spector, Brian spent more time on the floor of the studio than in the booth as he worked individually with each musician.

Once the takes began, the relationship between the participants remained organic. A famous example of this is found on Take 1 of the track to "God Only Knows" when the following exchanges occurred,

**Musician** [*believed to be Don Randi*] **to Brian** [*referring to the break between verses*]: "Hey Brian, why don't we do it short like this [*demonstrates*]".
**Brian:** "We'll try it".
**Musician to the others**: "Instead of playing the quarter note full, make it like a staccato note [*they try a run-through*]".
**Others:** "Yeah,… really enjoy it…"
**Brian:** "Yeah! In just that one spot! Wooooooooo!"

The resulting staccato on that small section is especially effective, even though it took up to Take 20 before Brian was satisfied. Towards the end of these takes, Brian's voice takes on a school-masterly air as he reins in the large, good humoured group of musicians assembled for that particular song.

With the cream of the Los Angeles session players at his disposal, Brian was ideally placed to fully develop the imaginative instrumental tracks he had produced for the *Today* album. Much of his previous work had centred upon developing guitar sounds unlike any of his contemporaries', and then using them sparsely on breaks or interjections between verses. The chopped but rounded sound, for example, on "Don't Worry Baby" had been extended on "Don't Hurt My Little Sister," "When I Grow Up" and others. Brian did not use guitars as lead instruments. Rather he aimed to include them in a specifically picked style within different combinations of instruments. Nothing about his use and sound of guitars was ever predictable or similar to other groups, and even with the surf guitar rooted break on "Dance, Dance, Dance," the sounds he achieved were distinctively richer and more original.

At this point, Brian's tracks sounded fuller than the works of his contemporaries because he adopted the Motown technique of binding songs together with percussion. Like many R & B producers, Brian plugged the gaps with tambourines, handclaps and alternative percussion instruments. Well before the baroque pop of The Left Banke, Brian was using harpsichord as a lead instrument in "When I Grow Up," and the instrument gained even further prominence on the *Pet Sounds* sessions. As indicated by his work with Hal Blaine, Brian developed an art of combining guitar, bass and drums with other families of instruments. For example, the background "drones" achieved with brass and woodwind on "Guess I'm Dumb" were continued, and added to with the integration of accordion and bass harmonica. Sometimes these were used as a layered background, however they often took more prominence as a lead group of sounds. Depth was also achieved more subtly with the use of traditional American instrumentation

© Capitol Photo Archives

*Brian directing from Western booth.*

like the tack piano, banjo and harmonicas. Brian's incorporation of such instruments evoked timbres and reference points that went far beyond the usual sonic ranges of popular music.

"Brian Wilson put all the strangest things together," Tom Petty comments, "guitars, banjo, harpsichord and maybe a harp all playing the same line so they created a really strange sound. It's not how any one thing sounds, but how the whole thing sounds."

The *Pet Sounds* sessions saw Brian stretch his powers of musical invention in a host of different ways: from the rule-breaking staccato use of accordions in "Wouldn't It Be Nice," to his use of bass harmonica duplicating expected sax lines. In fact, in many places it was extremely difficult to identify which instruments were being combined.

"There wasn't any way I could figure out what was playing," Danny

Hutton conceded. "And I didn't care what was playing. It was like going into sonic heaven."

One of the most striking sounds on the album was Brian's use of the theremin. In fact Brian came across this unusual instrument entirely by chance.

"It was one day at Western," explains David Kessel. "Brian was working in one room, and my dad [legendary session guitarist Barney Kessel] was working in the one next door with the theremin player Paul Tanner. Brian came in to ask my dad if he could make a session the next day, saw Paul's theremin, and asked what it was. He was really intrigued and immediately asked if the player could bring it to the next day's session."

In fact, the instrument Brian was so intrigued by wasn't actually a real theremin, as Tanner, a former trombonist with the legendary Glenn Miller Orchestra, explains.

"Well, I had encountered a real theremin some while before, and that of course is an instrument with which the player has no physical contact, aside from its magnetic fields. They are very, very tricky to play, and I thought 'I'm not going to play that! It's too hard!' So I set about making my own unit that would roughly duplicate the sound. What I had to do was to make it have more accuracy and consistency in the notes. It was an oscillator where you varied the pitch with a sort of wand! It became known as 'Paul's box', but it was not actually a theremin – simply an easier way of getting that sort of spacey sound. It was certainly interesting the way that Brian Wilson blended my sound with all the others."

This makeshift theremin was one of the most striking examples of Brian's use on *Pet Sounds* of instruments not well known by the majority of pop music listeners. The success of these experiments was facilitated by the willingness of the musicians to be inventive. Billy Strange recalls another example of Brian's unusual approaches to recording exactly what he wanted:

"Brian had a particular line that he wanted played on the bass pedals of the organ. He lay down on the floor and played the line for our keyboard player, Larry Knechtel, with his hands. Larry, a fine keyboardist, began playing the line with his feet as the take began and Brian came into the studio and stopped him. Brian had Larry lay on the floor, as he had, and Larry played the line to Brian's satisfaction. There was a certain feel that could only be attained by Larry playing the bass pedals with his hands, rather than his feet."

The magnificence of the *Pet Sounds* musical tracks can largely be attributed to Brian's imagination and inventiveness, but it should always be remembered that it was the skills and excellence of the session players that delivered the tracks. Brian, still very much their junior at age 23, had inspired them to join the expansive journey and their relationship of high mutual regard and respect led to a real milestone in pop.

Finally, the results of all Brian's complex experimentation and innovation on the backing tracks were mixed down onto one mono track in preparation for the vocals. Brian put down a guide lead on most of the tracks, saving his great love of the fully arranged background vocals for last. With the writing and track recording completed, Brian finally called on the other Beach Boys.

# Part II: We're Together Again: The Vocal Sessions

*"It's a very emotional record. Brian's voice at this point is so full of yearning and curiosity. Even though much of it has a melancholy tone, it always makes me feel good because I can relate to it both thematically and melodically. Sometimes there is comfort in feeling sad..."*

Brian Kassan (Ex-Wondermint)

*"Brian thinks in six-part harmony, instead of two or three part. He's not only a writer, he's an arranger and he has a concept of harmonics which is uncanny"*

Murry Wilson (Brian's dad, in a proud moment)

In a famous quote, ex-Raspberry Eric Carmen explained his long-term fascination with The Beach Boys' voices, "Their vocal harmonies are unsurpassed...I think Brian was a French Horn, Carl was a flute, Al Jardine a trumpet, Dennis a trombone, and Mike Love a baritone sax, before their incarnation as The Beach Boys."

© Capitol Photo Archives

*Mike Love at a separate mike, and Al in a raised position.*

"The Beach Boys are lucky...," Brian explained at the time. "We have a great range of voices; Mike can go from bass to the E above middle C; Dennis, Carl and Al progress upwards through C, A and B. I can take the second D in the treble clef."

For Brian, adding the vocals to the *Pet Sounds* backing tracks was *the* critical step. The voices were the key instruments in achieving his new musical vision. However, the owners of these instruments had some catching up to do.

While Brian began breaking new ground in Western Studios, the other Beach Boys – Mike, Al, Carl, Dennis and Bruce – had been off on a gruelling tour of Japan and Hawaii. Carl and Dennis had been kept up to date by phone calls from Brian during which he'd play acetates of some of the sessions. However, it is possible that Al and Mike may have felt somewhat apart from the project at the start. Although an earlier co-writer of "I'm Waiting For The Day," Mike was most conscious that the new songs were written with an outsider, which to him represented a radical new departure.

Bruce Johnston, himself an experienced producer, recalls when he realised that something important was happening:

"At first I wasn't really paying attention. I was into my XKE and girls! While we were away, it was mainly Carl and Dennis who were getting the bits from Brian. After the tour I sort of picked up on it mid-way through the instrumental recording when I took a girl to a session to show her what I was involved with. Well, there were about twenty musicians there, and as I listened I could hear that there was something really special happening. I started to drop into more sessions, and I remember the tracking session for 'God Only Knows' where there were so many crammed in with the rhythm and the strings. Wow! It was so very different!"

Once Bruce entered the studio, he began to comprehend the transition that the new material represented.

"As I watched Brian at work," he reflects, "I began to realise what was happening. We were all in changing times, musically and personally. Serious girls were becoming wives. There was a growing up happening. The Beatles had moved from 'She Loves You' to 'Norwegian Wood', and had made a whole cohesive album with *Rubber Soul*. Capitol saw this and so did Brian. He wanted to do just one story, and maybe this wasn't fully recognised by the others. I could see that Brian was connecting the dots!"

Brian praised *Rubber Soul,* as "a whole album with good stuff." This distinction between the Fabs previous US releases was crucial.

Apart from a Capitol re-release of early tracks, the two previous U.S. Beatles album releases in 1965 were *Beatles VI*, which was closest in content to the British *Beatles For Sale*, and *Help*, which also varied from the

British equivalent. Both albums were still rooted in the well constructed, but essentially straight-forward, pop songs that The Beatles had broken through with. The U.S. version of *Rubber Soul* was also different from the British release, but of more significance to Brian was the cohesive but more introspective mood of the songs. Partly lyrically reflective (as with "In My Life" and "Girl") and partly breaking new ground instrumentally (as with "Norwegian Wood"), the album would have given Brian many elements to ponder. Although *Rubber Soul* was issued in The States on 6th December 1965, probably too late to influence the writing of *Pet Sounds*, Brian would have heard it prior to the bulk of the recording. He was able to recognise that the goalposts had been moved by his competitors, and realised that he now had to respond.

For Bruce, the vocal recordings for *Pet Sounds* were the most difficult and the most fun Beach Boys sessions, with Brian drilling his singers like a military commander. Brian initially cut the lead vocal parts himself, some of which he kept and some of which he disregarded in favour of new leads from group members, most notably substituting his own voice for Carl's lovely, velvety lead on "God Only Knows". In the end, most of the leads were Brian; some were Mike and Carl, and the rest of the group took the backgrounds.

The group vocal parts began coming alive around the studio piano, where Brian showed the group their parts. The other Beach Boys rehearsed their parts, and then adjourned to the microphone to start balancing the sound. Mike Love was placed to the left on a separate microphone whilst the others

*© Capitol Photo Archives*

*Mike adds his great bass.*

gathered around two U 47s.

Brian explained the need to keep a constant distance between singer and mike, and tinkered with the individual distances till he was happy. Mike was isolated so that his less-powerful voice wasn't lost amongst the others. This also enabled him to concentrate on the tricky bass lines. Al Jardine, much to the amusement of the others, was sometimes perched up on an upturned crate so that the shorter Beach Boy could add his vocals at the same physical level as the others. Gathered around the mikes, facing each other or sometimes with their arms around each other, the group's takes could be spoilt by giggles or other noises, causing Brian to assume the role of the exasperated schoolmaster. He constantly made the group do parts over again, listening with a cocked ear to the front of a main studio speaker until he was satisfied.

"With 'Wouldn't It Be Nice,' we had to take several goes at it just to get the rhythm right," Bruce recalls. In fact, Brian went so far as to try this at his house on a four-track Scully recorder, to get the right sound. He even tried Dennis on bass.

"There were a few sour vocals, but eventually in the blend it's great," Bruce continues. "Brian would be out on the floor a lot. Chuck Britz would always get a brilliant and fat sound at Western where we did most of the vocals. He would give Brian choices whenever possible on the limited number of options available at that time. Since the end of World War Two, there has been equipment to make music sound great, but at *that* time there were not too many technical changes you could make. You could do a bit with EQ, limiting, delay and use the big live chambers. So the sound was what we made on the floor, not in the booth. Brian had to make decisions early on as there were so few tracks to play with."*

The band's then-publicist, the late Derek Taylor, captured the intensity and energy of the sessions in a contemporary article:

"Brian races from studio to control booth, in his efforts to be both singer and producer...not only must he manipulate the sounds which go down on tape, but the separate and unequal egos of The Beach Boys. They listen to

---

* While studio technology was moving quickly forward, both Brian's favourite studios, Western and Gold Star, had only four-track recording machines, which meant that Brian's recording possibilities were limited. For the preceding year or two, with the notable exception of his use of Colombia's new eight-track technology for "California Girls," Brian would record all the instrument tracks onto one of the four tracks and use the remaining three for the vocals. During the *Pet Sounds* sessions, with the help of studio engineers Chuck Britz and Larry Levine, Brian would sometimes use two four-track machines, subsequently transferring the results onto an eight-track machine. This would allow Brian seven tracks for vocal overdubs, as previously noted

*Brian and Mike.*

the tracks that Brian has spent hours recording. They listen in wonderment and awe. After swallowing the lumps in their throats and exchanging uneasy glances, work begins. First Bruce and Al step up to the mike to do the *dumdedums*, then Carl, Al and Dennis for the *runrunweeoos*. And Carl and Bruce for hums with Brian on falsetto. And on and on into the night, overdubbing, rearranging, softening, strengthening, shifting voices, moving Al farther away, Dennis back a step, Carl closer, Mike lower. Patiences wear out. Brian will accept nothing less than perfection."

On one occasion when Brian detected a particular miniscule discrepancy, Mike Love became frustrated. "Who's gonna hear that?" he cried, "You've got the ears of a dog!"

Indeed, the care that Brian put into the vocals showed how very special they were to Brian.

"The harmonies that we are able to produce give us a uniqueness," Brian explained, "which is really the only important thing you can put into records – some quality that no-one else has got. I love peaks in a song – and enhancing them on the control panel. Most of all, I love the human voice for its own sake..."

This love of the human voice grew out of those childhood evenings when Brian would teach his younger siblings simple harmonies in his bedroom. Those sessions took on their own special spiritual quality, serving as an oasis

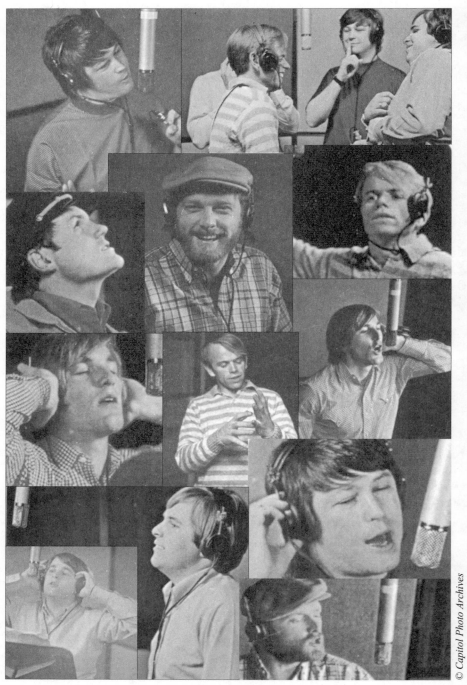

*Shots from the vocal sessions.*

© Capitol Photo Archives

*Brian joins in the backgrounds.*

of joy in the Wilson boys' turbulent lives. The simple act of group singing bound them together and provided what Carl saw as an almost religious outlet of love, "Recording had become church to us," he once mused.

In fact, during the *Pet Sounds* sessions Brian and Carl took part in prayers that Brian scribbled out. Brian had long shown an interest in religions and spiritualism in their widest forms, and his songwriting was now moving into deeper realms of self-examination and spiritual self-discovery. Never before had Brian's confidence been so high; never before had he felt so excited and so in control of his destiny.

Spurred on by this new found confidence, Brian took the *Pet Sounds* group vocals to a new high, with sections like the four bar drop-out on "Sloop John B," recorded in one take where the exuberant a capella vocals explode magnificently. Brian knew he could even build on these, and he did it. All the musicians were particularly struck by the magical "God Only Knows" session. For the vocal, Brian originally sang the comparatively simple lead, having in mind a particularly complex looping tag for the end fade.

"Brian called everyone and had them come down," Bruce Johnston explains. "He gave us all parts. There was Terry Melcher, Al, Mike, The Rovells and I and we did the tag. It was terrible – too cluttered, so Brian took it right back down to the clay. The eventual hit version only had three voices on it. In the centre section there is me, Carl and Brian, who takes the low line and also the high part, and then at the end tag it's just me answering Brian – just three parts on the whole thing."

The example of "God Only Knows" is telling. There are some parts of *Pet Sounds* that utilise all six members' voices. However compared to other Beach Boys' albums to this date, there were far fewer group backing vocals. Brian was crafting the vocals far more finely this time round, and leaving more space than before. Two tracks, "Caroline No" and "Don't Talk," have no background vocals, whilst "I'm Waiting For The Day" and "That's Not Me" are both vocally straightforward. Of the rest, backgrounds are often restricted to chorus sections and middle or end tags. Nonetheless, the discipline and complexity of the vocals on *Pet Sounds* is easily recognisable. Unlike The Beatles and The Rolling Stones, who bent vocals and took liberties without censure, The Beach Boys remained extremely structured, developing Brian's incredibly sophisticated vocal parts.

However, the process did not go entirely smoothly. It wasn't just Brian's perfectionism that irritated some members of the band. Although the work in progress was the new Beach Boys' album, Brian had written most of the music with a third party, recorded it with other musicians while the Beach Boys were mostly on tour, and now even dictated each of his fellow group members' vocal parts. Brian was aware that his almost total pre-determination of the backing vocal lines and their nuances of delivery caused upset and friction within the group, perhaps explaining Mike Love's reported reticence to attend all the vocal sessions. However, Brian appeared unable to compromise his vision.

"I think they thought it was for Brian Wilson only," Brian admitted a decade after *Pet Sounds*' release. "They knew that Brian Wilson was going to be a separate entity, something that was a force of his own, and it was generally considered that The Beach Boys were the main thing. So with *Pet Sounds* there was a resistance in that I was doing most of the artistic work on it vocally, and for that reason there was a little bit of inter-group struggle. It was resolved in the fact that they figured it was a showcase for Brian Wilson, but it was still The Beach Boys. In other words, they gave in. They let me have my little stint."

Bruce Johnston sums it up wryly, "*Pet Sounds* was the solo album that Brian shared with us."

✳︎✳︎ ✳︎✳︎✳︎✳︎

The final vocal sessions were probably completed in mid April 1966. By this time, Capitol was itching to get the finished article, and Brian was intensely aware of this time pressure when it came to mixing. The album was given extra body by the generous use of reverb to lift each track but it appears that the final mix down for the album was done in a rush, and

Brian's speed has been criticised for leading to a messy mix where some parts were hidden. Criticism has often been levelled at the studio noise that can be heard on Beach Boys' records, from whispering and chatting to audible coughs. Many tracks have been affected including "Surfin' USA," "Lonely Sea," "Little Deuce Coupe," "Custom Machine," "Louie Louie," "Ballad Of Old Betsy," "Wendy" and later on "Do It Again" and "How She Boogalood It". Other notable recording errors included doubling vocals, with slightly different words sung on each take, leading to a muddy, indistinct delivery, perhaps most easily noticed on "Shut Down". Such failings are probably best put down to the speed and pressure that the group was constantly under to quickly deliver more hit product. On *Pet Sounds*, studio background noise is most evident on the break of "Here Today". Unfortunately, as the interference was on the original mono mixdown of the instrumental track, it was not possible to take it out again later (a similar case being the bicycle bell on "You Still Believe In Me"). Still, songs with slight blemishes can become more acceptable to the listener than songs with "perfect" sound.

When the mixing was completed, Brian and an excited and proud Chuck Britz prepared the tapes for Capitol. The multi-track masters were retained by the group, as they always had been, and Capitol received the finished single mono tape. Artwork was then hastily prepared and Brian's twelfth Capitol album was ready to be pressed.

## Chapter 5
## NOW THAT EVERYTHING'S BEEN DONE:
## THE FINISHED ALBUM

© *Capitol Photo Archives*

*"I felt the production was a masterpiece.* Pet Sounds *was an offshoot of the Phil Spector production technique. I'm proud of it for that reason, in that we were able to produce tracks that had a monumental sound to them...It wasn't really a song concept album or lyrically a concept album...It was really a production concept album."* – Brian Wilson, 1976.

*"'Pet Sounds' blew me out of the water...I loved the album so much. I've just bought my kids each a copy of it for their education in life – I figure no one is educated musically 'til they've heard that album...It is better than ever (now)."* – Paul McCartney, 1990.

The reaction of existing Beach Boys' fans when they first heard *Pet Sounds* has often been described as a mixture of bewilderment and surprise. Certainly the music was not the catchy, accessible pop that listeners were used to. In its place was a fully realised collection of delicately crafted songs with new sonorities and moods that required real concentration to hear and appreciate. It demanded an approach that simply hadn't ever been necessary for a pop long player up to that point – one that would not only affect the listener, but every musician's approach to the idea of making an album. It was a treasure chest so full of gems that it was impossible to comprehend fully in one or even several listens. As well as the magnificent whole, each individual track was demanding of an appreciation that was frankly beyond the musical vocabulary of most fans in 1966. Still, it was the whole that was the key!

However, whilst all evidence points towards Brian consciously writing a set of songs about the more adult themes of relationships, it is less obvious that his original idea for *Pet Sounds* was a fully formed concept album. Nonetheless, the tracks eventually chosen by Brian to form the core of the album allow a lyrical concept to be identified. Writer Neal Umphred described the album's core as "Ten interrelated songs that dealt with the transition from the innocence of first love to the self conscious reflection of experience." Bruce Johnston acknowledged such a concept when he suggested that "Good Vibrations" could have fitted well early on Side One, as part of the rush of excitement experienced in blossoming relationships. Long-time Beach Boys U.S. expert Peter Reum saw the work as "A kaleidoscope of emotions", and in a similar vein writer David Leaf interpreted the suite of songs as "the emotional conflicts facing a young man...on the cusp of adulthood."

The desire to move away from the 'traditional' areas of Beach Boys material was strong, but perhaps was not as far away as it could have been. Whilst others around him in America, Dylan, P.F. Sloan and much of the folk rock movement, were writing material that addressed the world around them, Brian was seeking to address adolescent and young adult relationship issues. Tony Asher later observed that he thought that *Pet Sounds* took Brian himself through a form of adolescence, so it could be conjectured that he would not have been ready to write about world issues. His highly demanding career of the previous four years had kept him isolated from current affairs.

Brian's work described his own situation and his own weighty responsibilities eloquently whilst perfectly capturing the bittersweet journey of adolescence. The album's long-standing appeal has shown that it strikes a universal chord and provides solace to many at times when emotional support is needed. Brian, in an interview for *The Telegraph* Magazine in 1995, identified one of the key themes, when he recalled the sad and reflective end to the album with "Caroline No",

"Oh it was (sad), but you know life goes on. So you get knocked on your butt. I got knocked on my butt a couple of times, but you get back up and you keep working. I mean, like there's always the chance of a better day. Giving up is only for idiots. Only idiots give up, you know."

From the opening song "Wouldn't It Be Nice", an innocent teen's wish to be old enough to wake up next to his sweetheart, Brian sets out his stall with a range of subtle tempo shifts, complicated vocal patterns and a blend of inventive instrumentation. Sandy Salisbury, ex-Ballroom/Millennium member and Curt Boettcher collaboraor, sees it as the ultimate Beach Boys creation, "It has all the elements of what they were to me – melody and harmony, happy lyrics and sunny days. Top of the radio, soul of feel-good music. If you want to know The Beach Boys, that tune paints their portrait." The song's memorable pretty opening three bars of guitar doubled with harp is shattered with a huge drum strike on the first note of the fourth bar, ushering in the first verse. Already, with this dramatic opener, Brian shows that the drums and percussive effects have more than a walk-on part in this epic. Brandt Huseman, who together with his brother Matt formed Splitsville and recorded a recent album called *Pet Soul*, particularly appreciates the percussion, "I love the 'talking' drum parts after the bridge," Huseman says, "when, right before it goes back into the chorus, the snare drum and timpani answer each other. It's a cool effect!"

The accordions, as well as adding an unusually textured sound, carry much of the internal rhythm of the track, and dropping them out on the middle section allows the guitar to provide a shimmering feel. Also introduced are the rasping saxes, as used on "Guess I'm Dumb," which act as a bottom end and contrast to the lighter guitar figures. They blend beautifully with guitar and accordions just over a minute into the song, providing one of the sublime combinations that characterise the album. The youthful quality of Brian's verse lead tops off this stunning opener.

Tony Asher remembers his son especially relating to "Wouldn't It Be Nice". It's a song that communicates easily and effectively to youth in any decade, but perhaps even more poignantly on post-Aids generations.

The mood changes for the second song "You Still Believe In Me," with its more mature themes of devotion and frailty – "*I try hard to be strong, but sometimes I fail myself*". The delicacy of relationships is echoed in the arrangement that interweaves the instruments in a gossamer mix highlighted by finger cymbals. Everything is gently restrained, and the incongruity of a bicycle bell and a bulb horn serve to catch the listener's closer attention. Brian's tender lead is boosted by the group unison vocals on the title, and the "*I want to cry*" end tag introduces another musical motif, with the vocals following gradually descending notes. These descents can be found in more obvious patterns on the bass guitar elsewhere on the album, most notably on "Here Today."

"That's Not Me" reveals a sensitive soul far removed from the super-confident fun-loving persona of the Beach Boys' earlier hits, as the protagonist admits his feelings of insecurity: "*I had to prove that I could make it alone, now, but that's not me/ I wanted to show how independent I'd grown, now but that's not me.*" In direct contrast to the "two girls for every guy" dream of an earlier hit, what really matters to the singer is what he "*could be to just one girl*".

Ironically, the most sensitive lyric so far features Mike Love's first lead vocal on the album, although he is joined by Brian on the bridge. The busy tambourine-led percussion and distinct drums over the held organ line allow vocal prominence as Love describes the uncertainties of growing up. The song is characterised by the unusual key changes that caused Tony Asher some difficulties with the lyrics. The wandering bass line complements the verses well, and the restrained guitar updates the rich sound first heard on "Don't Worry Baby." The backing vocals gently build, injecting clipped punctuation with single held notes before dropping out completely at the end. "That's Not Me" is one of the better examples of the surprising musical twists and turns that cause musicians to value Brian's work so highly.

The emotional heart of side one of the album is track four, "Don't Talk (Put Your Head On My Shoulder)". British musician Sean Macreavy perceives this is literal terms, "The wonderful '*listen, listen*' passage, where the acoustic bass descends arm-in-arm with the ride cymbal, cellos and violas can only be a heartbeat, and it is heart-stopping." The song serves as a statement of conscious romanticism. It arose directly from Brian and Asher's intimate discussions, and deals with the extra dimensions of love found in non-verbal communication. Brian was proud of the "innocence of youth" in his double-tracked voice that delivered the song without any supporting vocals. The held organ notes give a hymnal foundation for Brian's falsetto. The strings were added separately, and they enhance the track dramatically. Elsewhere on the album, Brian achieves depth through reverb-enriched percussion; here it is created by the blend of strings, as the cello and viola anchor the violins to give a rich shimmering texture.

"I love the way he uses strings on this album," Pearlfishers leader, David Scott, enthuses, "–quite sparingly and usually with quite a small section. It's more normal for pop records to use larger sections but on *Pet Sounds,* when the strings come you can hear the character of each part." Though they were not involved with the co-operative construction of Brian's tracks, the string players adjusted well to rock and pop, and with these sessions they successfully contributed another colour to Brian's palette.

*Pet Sounds* is often built with sonic contrasts, and nowhere is this more overt than on "I'm Waiting For The Day," a beautiful song about comforting someone with a broken heart and waiting for them to be able to love again, which is constructed to match gentleness with stridency in both the vocals and instrumental track. Brian's lead is appropriately restrained when he sings *"You needed someone to help forget about him,"* and suitably sharper on *"You didn't think, that I would sit around and let him take you."*

"For the most part, the lead is a beautifully, sweetly sung and completely convincing performance," says British harmony king Tony Rivers. "It's a song that modulates through some haunting string parts into what almost feels like a 'false' ending, but then doubles tempo with Brian really rocking out on the lyric."

The tenor of the background vocals is also rawer as "*ooos*" are replaced by "*aaahs*," and Mike Love resorts to his "goofy" bass, making the whole supporting vocal framework less smooth round the edges than elsewhere. Huge drums and timpani – the biggest anywhere on the album – introduce an organ that immediately transforms to a delicate skipping backdrop for a horn supporting the broken-hearted lyrics. Flutes enter to introduce a new motif, and they remain to echo the vocal line in the chorus before they take up the melody with a time shift in yet another section. The wandering bass guitar now enhances the final climax with repeated descending runs that contribute to the overall sense of unease.

The patience in the lyric, and the tone of consideration for the beloved's needs rather than the fulfilment of one's own desires, in lines such as *"I know you cried and you felt blue/But when I could, I gave strength to you"*, make this a particularly mature achievement. Such empathy was rare in the pop of the time.

After "I'm Waiting For The Day," as if to give a respite from the emotional rollercoaster ride that he has given listeners thus far, Brian inserts an instrumental interlude appropriately entitled "Let's Go Away For Awhile." Without the Capitol-inspired inclusion of "Sloop John B" which follows it, this track would have finished side one and provided a timely pause. Gentle vibes and guitar create a relaxed platform for a simple, effective melody, while saxophones and strings blend seamlessly. Brian, who has always referred to this track with particular pride, apparently wrote lyrics for it, but in the end, opted to leave them out.

"'Let's Go Away For Awhile' is the most satisfying piece of music I have ever made," Brian insisted. "I applied a certain set of dynamics through the arrangement and the mixing and got a full musical extension of what I had planned during the early stages of the theme. I think the chord changes are very special. I used a lot of musicians on the track – twelve violins, piano, four saxes, oboe, vibes, a guitar with a Coke bottle on the strings for a semi-steel guitar effect. Also I used two basses and percussion. The total effect is…let's go away for awhile…nice thought! Most of us don't go away, but it's still a nice thought. It stands up well alone."

The final track of side one of the original vinyl, The Beach Boys' version of the traditional folk song "Sloop John B," has no lyrical or mood connection with the rest of the album, but nevertheless holds its head high in terms of vocal and instrumental quality. Leading off with Brian's doubled lead, the vocals achieve their full effect when the group joins in counterlines. Here is a fine example of how enriching Mike Love's lower registers can be. The wonderful culmination of different vocal lines near the end provides the best-ever example of the group's vocal talents. The instrumental track is constructed in a similar way. Delicate flute and tinkling percussion introduce the melody before being joined by guitar and glockenspiel. A simple drum pattern and a walking bass line build to the entry of the low droning saxes, which anchor the backing track much as Love anchors the vocal blend. The flute is re-introduced with sustained notes as the drum and bass counter each other in the final swell.

"Sloop John B," recorded months before most of the others, is also a good example of how Brian developed his use of the electric guitar. Whereas most producers would have used strummed chords on this song, Brian opts for high picked notes, distinguishing *Pet Sounds* from other contemporary works.

Side two of the original LP opens with "God Only Knows", the prettiest love song on the album. However, even amidst the central conceit there is the consideration – albeit dismissed – of self-doubt: "*I may not always love you / But as long as there are stars above you /You never need to doubt it.*" Certainly the refrain "*God only knows what I'd be without you*" marks a vulnerability and maturity miles ahead of the earlier paeans to fun in the sun.

Brian's sound construction also gives the track an unforgettable delicacy. It had an immediate effect on Margo Guryan, whose gentle *Take A Picture* album was written as a direct result of hearing the song.

"To say that my life changed in two minutes, 46 seconds would not be exaggerating," Margo insists. "It taught me how songs could be structured by allowing the bassline to determine the chord choice rather than the other way round. I listened to it over and over again, learned the words, sang with it, immersed myself in it, and I began to understand. I sat down at my electric piano and wrote 'Think Of Rain.' It seemed to drift out of me with no help from my head or hands."

"God Only Knows" is characterised by light instrumental touches that punctuate and complement the vocals and make the track shimmer. Led by gentle accordions and a haunting French horn, sleigh bells and percussion form a romantic backdrop, allowing the strings and saxophones to take centre stage. The suggestion of staccato on the break serves to reinforce the emotional delight, while once again the percussion provides part of the bed for the vocals.

"Such percussion's standard use resides as a theatrical device for mimicking a comedian's gait," comments songwriter Peter Lacey. "But here, such corny percussion blends sublimely into the mix, as if angels had exchanged them for their harps."

Carl's gentle lead vocal perfectly complements the track, and the fugue break and choice of reverting to simpler answering vocal loops on the fade reinforce the old adage of "less is more." Indeed, Brian tried and rejected full group vocals.

"God Only Knows" would become the most covered song on the album. Those who have recorded it include, PP Arnold, David Bowie, Glen Campbell, Neil Diamond, Justin Hayward and the London Symphony Orchestra, as well as more modern versions by Elvis Costello & the Brodsky Quartet, Teenage Fan Club and Gary Numan.

Side two, track two, "I Know There's An Answer", which predates Tony Asher's involvement, appears acutely autobiographical, in spite of Mike Love's additional lyrical input. The singer appears to be consciously rejecting a retreat to the comfort of his own isolation – in his room, or wherever – as a solution to his problems: "*I know so many people who think they can do it alone / They isolate their heads and stay in their safety zone.*"

The backing track blends guitars with piano and organ to provide a light cushion for the vocals, with rasping sax and bass harmonica once again acting as a contrast. However, this track is a good example of session sheets failing to tell the full story of the session; instrumental credits seem to be missing. The sheets credit drums – Hal Blaine adds tom toms to accent the chorus – tambourine – the track's main source of percussion – Fender bass, string bass, guitars, piano, organ, saxophones and bass harmonica, but there also appears to be a hidden flute that probably would have been played by Jim Horn.*

The lead vocals are unusually split three ways: Mike begins in a low register for the first two lines of the verse, followed by Al for the later ones. Then Brian takes the repeated chorus line *"I know there's an answer/ I know now but I had to find it by myself,"* which encapsulates much of the sentiment of the entire album.

"Here Today" offers the pessimistic view that *"Love is here today / And it's gone tomorrow"*. The track's bass lines have provoked much interest, and Paul McCartney has admitted to being particularly influenced by them. Brian purposefully used Ray Pohlman's bass guitar an octave higher than normal to create more of a driving feel. Key changes and tempo shifts characterise the track, which uses striking descending flourishes from bass and trombone on the chorus against a simple organ figure and strummed guitar. Mike Love sings a strong lead with a group chorus, making this one of the most accessible tracks to Beach Boys fans apart from "Wouldn't It Be Nice" and "Sloop John B."

"All Brian's vocal influences are there in the arrangements," Tony Rivers comments, "such as The Four Freshmen parts on "You Still Believe In Me" and "Here Today" through Doo Wop and even 'barbershop' 7ths scattered throughout."

"Here Today" was one of the first *Pet Sounds* tracks to attract a cover in Britain – by The Robb Storme Group. The *Sessions* Box Set also reveals the conversation about cameras that famously muddies the instrumental break.

"I Just Wasn't Made For These Times" is another song that sounds acutely autobiographical as Brian confesses over and over again *"Sometimes I feel very sad."*

Dismissing "fair weather friends", the protagonist is *"looking for a place to fit in, where I can speak my mind."* Although Tony Asher wrote the final lyric, it was directly as a response to Brian wanting to come up with a song about not fitting in.

"I think that we captured an emotion that many people feel for different reasons," Asher comments. However, the song can also be interpreted as being about Brian's own perceived place within The Beach Boys. *"Every time I get the inspiration to go change things around,"* Brian would sing, *"No one wants to help me look for places where new things might be found."* These words are strangely appropriate to the lone, inspired musical

---

* It has long been suspected that the existing *Pet Sounds* session sheets may not tell the whole story of the musicians involved. Whilst they are certainly broadly correct, Hal Blaine confirms that errors and omissions, whilst unlikely, could have occurred. This is thought to be more likely on the larger sessions.

experimentation that was taking Brian far beyond his group.

"I Just Wasn't…"'s backing track is constructed to give the picked bass another prominent role against a background blend of piano, harpsichord and (again uncredited) banjo. The saxes and harmonica provide an alternative musical undercurrent, with pauses filled with flute and lovely echoing temple blocks. The "theremin" takes on a falsetto vocal quality towards the end as it weaves in and out of the background.

The song is perhaps one of the best examples of Brian's evocative sound-blending. Musician Sean Macreavy describes the results as sonic cocktails. "These cocktails are the very glue that binds the album together," Macreavy remarks, "'I Just Wasn't Made For These Times' has the plucked Fender bass floating airily alongside Hal Blaine's blocks and a playful ukulele; baritone saxes are welded to cor anglais and oboe; acoustic bass to bass harmonica. In the strange world of marital bliss that is *Pet Sounds*, no sound is single."

Finally, Brian's doubled lead vocal contrasts the complicated dual group vocal lines on the choruses.

The instrumental track "Pet Sounds," dating back to sessions conducted during the previous November, is a great collage of sound that balances the relaxed feel on "Let's Go Away For Awhile." It also vividly illustrates Brian's explorations of new guitar and percussion sounds. Woodblocks and a soda can being struck combine with the guiro and sleigh bells, while a winding, hypnotic guitar figure provides the song with a weepy sound.

"Caroline No," which does not have any contribution from the other Beach Boys, is a bold choice for the album's closer. Brian has often cited it as his favourite track, perhaps because it was the nearest he had got to a true solo project. But, it was the melody rather than the arrangement that Brian would often rhapsodise. "It totally consists of notes that don't sound like they're bunched together," Brian pointed out. "They sound like they flow together. The better the flow, the better the melody."

Nancy Sinatra, who loved the album, would later single out this song for particular praise.

"*Pet Sounds*…I love it, I *treasure* it!" Nancy insists. "I include 'God Only Knows' in my set, but my favourite song from it is 'Caroline No.' Brian articulates his feelings so beautifully on the album and that track particularly that I am moved to tears."

On one level, "Caroline No" is a finely crafted, bittersweet meditation on a love that has died: "*Where is the girl I used to know? … Could I ever find in you again /Things that made me love you so much then?/ Could we ever bring 'em back once they have gone?/ Oh, Caroline No.*" However, the narrator's heart wasn't broken by Caroline's unfaithfulness, but by the fact that she changed, cut her hair short, and grew up. The song represents the final step in *Pet Sounds'* pilgrim's progress from the innocence epitomised by the teenage longing for adult love in "Wouldn't It Be Nice", to this more sober state of experience.

"This is definitely one of the songs that was reflective of our moods," Asher explains. "We were looking back, perhaps at simpler times with less pressure. I had a personal story linked to that song. I had broken up with a girl called Carol some while before, and I wrote the song linked to our mood with her in mind. The original lyric was *'Oh Carol, I know,'* which was in a song about a girl who was going through changes and inevitable growing up. Brian heard it as *'Caroline No,'* which actually seemed more interesting to me. My original plan had been for the song to be answering and agreeing with the inevitability of growing and sometimes moving away. And yes, my Carol had cut her hair after she had moved away. Some people think that it was a personal song about Marilyn, who I believe had also cut her hair, but it really came out of our mood and my experiences."

The song features Brian's doubled vocal against a floating bed of guitar, harpsichord and ukulele. Carol Kaye's strong bass guitar and the punctuating percussion are prominent, while the saxophones are much more restrained than on other tracks. Gentle vibes, enhanced by the combination of flute and bass flute, contribute to the ethereal quality and the wistful feel of the lyrics.

The record finishes with the sound of a train passing by and disappearing into the distance, and the sound of dogs – Brian's beagle, Banana, and his weimaraner, Louie – barking. It's appropriate that one of the last things the listener hears on *Pet Sounds*, is the sound of Brian's pets! As the train noise subsides, it is as if the whole album pauses for a moment of reflection. The listener looks back before the audible train passes on, giving an almost cinematic moment after the aural highs. The purpose of train sound has been discussed and analysed: it might have been an aural metaphor, or it might just have been a track on a sounds effect disc that Brian just happened to like. Brian has been quoted as seeing himself standing at the back of the train as it passes, perhaps moving on after completing his job, and letting the final moment be his alone.

*Pet Sounds* was always intended to be a thought provoking experience, from the nature of its lyrics, its ground breaking instrumental blends and its radical place within the Beach Boys canon. Brian Wilson purposefully set out to achieve such a new experience, and he succeeded beyond his wildest dreams. However, whilst it would remain a body of work which would deeply affect future generations of musicians and fans, its initial reception would be substantially different to what Brian might have imagined.

His then wife Marilyn, some ten years on in a piece for *Rolling Stone* magazine, recalled the whole episode,

"Boy, he worked his butt off when he was making *Pet Sounds*. And I'll never forget the night that he finally got the final disc, when they finished it, dubbing it down and all that, and he brought the disc home. And he prepared a moment. We went in the bedroom, we had a stereo in the bedroom, and he goes, 'OK, are you ready?' But he was really serious – there was his soul in there, you know? And we just lay there alone all night, you know, on the bed, and just listened and cried. It was really, really heavy.

"But *Pet Sounds* was not a big hit. That really hurt him badly, he couldn't understand it. It's like, why put your heart and soul into something? I think that had a lot to do with slowing him down."

# Chapter 6
## THE ALBUM ARRIVES

© *Capitol Photo Archives*

*Brian at San Diego Zoo.*

*"Brian took me into another room and said that The Beach Boys were a strange group; he said they had neglected many things, like artwork and pictures and press, but that now things had a shape and form and direction he could recognise and describe, he didn't want things to get away from them. He wanted everything to come together. We decided to have new pix taken, simple things in fields – without the striped shirts – and we decided not to beat around the bush anymore."* – Derek Taylor (Publicist)

*"Got the first copy right before school started for me at Fairfax from Wallich's Music City in Hollywood. $3.99. In monoaural. In 1967 I did a term paper in a Lit class on* Pet Sounds *– just about everybody in the room laughed at me."* Harvey Kubernik (L.A. Writer/Producer)

On 16th May 1966, *Pet Sounds* was released in the U.S. as Capitol T 2458. It was packaged in a cute sleeve depicting The Beach Boys (sans Bruce, who was kept out of the main shots for contractual reasons) in the petting corner of the San Diego Zoo with half a dozen goats. The three Wilson brothers and Al are feeding the animals bits of apple, whilst Mike Love surveys the scene from behind. The group name, title and track listing come out of a grass-green background, with "Sloop John B" and "Caroline No" as the featured tracks having both been issued as singles. The rear of the cover was in black and white, and featured shots from the Japanese tour and a variety of stage and casual shots (which do include Bruce). Two different fonts are featured on the back, including a rustic, made-from-rough-wood lettering for the album title and tracks, which was possibly originally chosen for the main font. A single shot of Brian in the top left corner dominates the back cover; he sits pensively at a piano.

The inner sleeve of the first issues was the usual advertising opportunity for

*The petting corner.*

other Capitol product. Brian's new music arrived in a sleeve strangely featuring only two other Beach Boys albums, two Beatles, two Lettermen, one Peter & Gordon, but another forty seven covering the main catalogue of show tunes, easy country stars and established stars like Nat King Cole and Nancy Wilson. These inner sleeves were changed reasonably regularly, so it is hard to understand why Capitol had not designed a pop one just featuring their unit-shifting hot acts by this stage. How many Beatles and Beach Boys fans were also likely to be buying Liza Minnelli and Jackie Gleason? Still, with this obvious anomaly aside, the album design generally reflected that this was different Beach Boys territory, with no striped shirts or chrome in sight.

At Capitol Records, Brian had developed a good friendship with A&R executive Karl Engemann. Initially working as a producer, Engemann moved across to the business side as the group arrived, and became the company link to Brian and his family. Engemann was supportive of Brian's work and regularly visited him to see where it was heading. When he heard the new album, Engemann realised two things: its musical worth and its originality. It was certainly the latter that the Capitol sales team noticed first. Where, they asked, was the easily digested mass-market material? The subtlety and musicality of the album was lost on them, as their outlook was geared to the easily-shifting units that past Beach Boys' product had provided. Certainly the complex and sophisticated new record would prove a far harder sell.

"I thought Brian was screwing up," Nick Venet, the Beach Boys' former producer, commented on the album. "He was no longer looking to make records, he was looking for attention from the business. He was trying to torment his father with songs his father couldn't relate to and melody

© Capitol Photo Archives

*The striped shirts are outgrown.*

structures his father couldn't understand." Brian certainly had what he later described as an "industry hit", though it is doubtful that this was his prime motivation. Similarly, the idea that he was purposefully tormenting his father should be seen as incidental at worst when set against his stated goal of making the best album ever and his spiritual desire to spread love around.

The album entered the U.S.chart of 28th May at Number 106 and peaked at 10 by 2nd July. This was a respectable sales performance, but it was a drop from the *Concert* album, which had topped the charts 18 months before. The album's progress was slowed by a chart clogged with a welter of material from the likes of Herb Albert's Tijuana Brass, Lou Rawls and Bill Cosby, as well as the *Sound of Music* and *Dr. Zhivago* soundtracks. The Mamas And Papas' debut was the only real pop record higher on the charts than *Pet Sounds*.

*A British EP release.*

In terms of singles, the atypical "Sloop John B" peaked in the U.S. at Number 3 in early May before dropping off the charts by June 11th . Brian's solo-marketed single, "Caroline No" was less successful, peaking in April at Number 32. The period between June 18th and July 23rd had no Beach Boys singles releases until "Wouldn't It Be Nice" entered at Number 84 rising to 8 by mid-September. Its B-side, "God Only Knows," followed a week later but stalled at 39 on 24 September. Initially, the single had "God Only Knows" as the plug side, but disquiet about the word God in the title amongst radio personnel, store owners and Capitol's sales team led to the disc being rapidly flipped.

© Capitol Photo Archives

*An album ad in a Beach Boys music book.*

At Capitol's Hollywood headquarters, the sceptical sales team was vindicated by *Pet Sounds*' poor chart showing. The Capitol reps were used to typical Beach Boys albums easily achieving Top 5 status. The relatively poor sales of the new record told Capitol's marketing team that it was time for a greatest hits package to reclaim the lost ground. A *Best Of The Beach Boys* collection originally scheduled for later in the year was quickly brought forward and issued on July 5th, less than two months after *Pet Sounds*. Surprisingly, this hits album remained on the charts for only nine weeks, peaking at Number 8. However, Capitol continued its unimaginative sales policy by releasing a *Best Of The Beach Boys, Vol. 2* in July 1967, which peaked at Number 50, and a third hits package in August 1968, which reached no higher than 153. Engemann sadly admits that sales force pressure was probably to blame for Capitol's failure to promote *Pet Sounds*. Had Capitol recognised the album as a masterpiece and supported it, Brian's life in the period directly after its release might have followed a happier and more creative path.

Still, the fact remains that, although it only just made the Top 10, *Pet Sounds* was very far from being a sales failure, shifting some 200,000 copies pretty rapidly. Sales could have been significantly higher – even approaching the half million suggested in Steven Gaines' *Heroes and Villains* – had Capitol not taken to fulfilling re-orders of *Pet Sounds* with copies of *Best Of The Beach Boys*!

Sales were no doubt aided by the high visibility of the group in the teen mags at the time, like *16*, *Tiger Beat* and the Capitol backed *Teenset*. The latter mag was constantly behind the band, getting exclusive photo shoots and articles, through the contacts made by the mature first editor Earl Leaf, and the subsequent much younger editor, the ubiquitous and imaginative Judy Sims.

✳ ✳ ✳ ✳ ✳

By the time *Pet Sounds* was released, the English pop scene had been dominating the world's music charts for a couple of years, and the Beach Boys' publicist Derek Taylor, an Englishman living in Hollywood, who had previously acted on behalf of The Beatles, was well aware of this. He saw Hollywood as an extension of London. To maintain the link, he regularly supplied a column to the English pop weekly *Record Mirror*. Through Taylor's weekly column, British fans were kept informed of what was happening in L.A. – for many a welcome relief from the Brit-beat overkill. Taylor knew that a good British reception for *Pet Sounds* could help the album in other markets too, so he set about some extremely targeted marketing.

"I had a chance to go to Britain, as there was so much interest in the group at that time," Bruce Johnston explains. "The U.K. was mad about us! We had enjoyed good success there since 'I Get Around' had gone Top 10. Mick Jagger had taken that record to some of the pirate stations and helped to break it. It was to be my first trip there, and the trip was sort of turned into marketing by Derek Taylor. I had originally planned to just go and hang out. I hadn't gone planning interviews, but the whole thing evolved at the speed of light. Kim Fowley, who I had known since the fifties, was over there already and apparently Derek called him up to help. It turned out that he was to act as a sort of traffic policeman!"

"I was a weird guy from Hollywood, living and working in Britain at the time," says Fowley. "I was 26 and 27 but looked 19 or 21, and I was having a great time! I was producing people like The In-Betweens before they were Slade, The Belfast Gypsies and Cat Stevens. Anyway, Derek figured that I was in the centre of things..."

Taylor installed Bruce in a suite at London's Waldorf Hotel, a traditional wood panelled hotel in Aldwych, and invited the British press to come and listen to *Pet Sounds*.

"The Waldorf was a careful choice," Fowley explains. "It was definitely *not* a rock and roll hotel! The visiting press would see and pass by vast wealth, and they would arrive and be treated to a steak dinner with champagne. Every hour we would change guys – we always had a queue of reporters and we sure kept the waiters running! It was a great concept with everyone being in a very *classy* mood. We had a record player in the room, and Bruce was able to bask in the rapture. Bruce is smart and cultured, and he knew his way round the press guys and he was well able to avoid any minefields."

Before long, the British press were referring to Bruce reverentially as the "Beach Boys' ambassador in tennis shoes."

Meanwhile, British harmony singer Tony Rivers, suggested Taylor contact Who drummer, and Beach Boys fan, Keith Moon.

"I met Keith Moon, who was the coolest guy," Bruce recalls. "He loved all our stuff and all West Coast harmony music... Keith attracted people, and he became a fantastic tour guide. Many, many people came to the hotel to hear the album, and I must have played it so many times... and we saw lots of press people and the stars of the day."

Keith took Bruce and friends to a Tony Rivers and The Castaways gig in Romford where Keith and Bruce joined in a somewhat chaotic set, much to the delight of the surprised audience. Another night, Keith took them to a local Who gig which involved two limos: one with Bruce, Kim, Keith and John Entwistle the other with Pete Townshend and Roger Daltrey. Even

Kim blanches at the memory of bumping and mutual attempts at forcing off the road, but they lived to see the next day and more press visits.

"Keith was seeing himself on a missionary quest," says Fowley. "He was wild, but he had good ears and a good heart. He thought *Pet Sounds* was going to change the world. He was the best messenger out into the community, as he had access everywhere... Keith arranged that after the press people came the celebrities. There were plenty of chairs around the room, and an alcove so we could see who was coming and going. Believe me, we kept the bar going."

"The men and women from the press were very courteous," Bruce recalls. "I remember Keith Altham (*NME*) as a charming man, and Penny Valentine being sweet. The tone of the music paper writing was positive then, and not angry...."

One evening at the Waldorf Hotel, two other visitors named John Lennon and Paul McCartney, dressed up in their Beatles stage suits for the occasion, came by. Once Lennon and McCartney had settled in with drinks, they got down to the serious business of the visit. "They wanted to hear *Pet Sounds*," says Bruce. "They called for the room to be silent, which it was, and they listened to it straight through twice in silence. They were thrilled! We spent maybe three hours together. I was the hero who took no bows!"

"I don't recall who it was, but someone asked for a piano after they had listened to the album, and one was wheeled in," says Fowley. "There were smiles all round, and a kind of a buzz. John and Paul went to the piano, sort of whispering together, and started to play some chords. After a little while, they said goodbye and sent messages to people, especially Brian, and they went off with Keith. They said simply, 'We'll tell everybody!'"

Interestingly, Andrew Loog Oldham, The Rolling Stones' manager at that time, reckons McCartney had already heard the album.

"Lou Adler [legendary L.A. record producer linked to P.F.Sloan, Jan & Dean, The Mamas And Papas and Dunhill Records] arrived in town with an acetate of *Pet Sounds*. He came to my house from London Airport. I sat in smoke with Paul McCartney and that first listen changed our lives..."

The possibility that the Waldorf visit was not McCartney's first listening of the album intrigued Bruce when I put it to him. He immediately put in a call to Adler. Lou was adamant that the evening at Loog Oldham's was the first time McCartney had heard *Pet Sounds*, and told Bruce that there was much discussion about which ideas The Beatles could pinch from the album. The Waldorf meeting appears almost certainly to involve an already converted McCartney evangelically bringing Lennon to hear it for the first time. This would underline the impact that the album had on McCartney. The Beatles' interest and competitive spirit had been awakened, and their eventual issue of *Sgt. Pepper* as a conceptual album has always been correctly traced back to the cohesiveness and ambition of *Pet Sounds*. More specifically, McCartney has been quoted as saying that immediately on hearing the album, he went off and wrote "Here There and Everywhere."

The next day at the Waldorf, after a few more visitors (probably including Paul and Barry Ryan with *Top Of The Pops* girl Samantha Juste, and then popular duo The Merseys), Bruce paid the bill, and the three-day promotional foray was over. The net result of the trip was plenty of word of mouth amongst hip circles and a lot of very positive column inches in the press, so that when the album was released in June – just over a month after the American release – it was received with open British arms.

"Just out in America is a brand new spanking hot Beach Boys LP called *Pet Sounds*," Penny Valentine enthused in a special boxed trailer in *Disc and Music Echo*. "Thirteen tracks of Brian Wilson genius, packaged in a nice cover of The Beach Boys looking benignly at some pretty hungry pastel goats. Each track has that lovely distinctive smothered Wilson sound as though they're all singing through sugar cotton wool. The whole LP is far more romantic than the usual Beach Boys jollity. Sad little wistful songs about lost love and found love and all around love."

The album crashed into the British *NME* chart at Number 6 on 9th July 1966. The preceding few months had been dominated by the sales of *The Sound Of Music* soundtrack, which had given way only to The Beatles' *Rubber Soul* and The Rolling Stones' *Aftermath*. Although *Pet Sounds* never toppled *The Sound Of Music* from the top spot, it produced long-lasting, strong sales, then unprecedented for an American group. From Number 6 it climbed to Number 2, remaining in the top 5 for an amazing eighteen weeks, and only dropped out of the top 10 just before Christmas. Meanwhile, *The Best Of The Beach Boys* also cemented the group's reputation arriving at Number 5 on 12th November. It too rose straight to 2 for several weeks, remaining Top 10 for over a full year. At the end of 1966 the *NME* poll announced that The Beach Boys had managed to topple The Beatles from their "Top World Group" status. The Beach Boys' stock in Britain was never higher, and it had been achieved almost entirely on the strength of their music.

It was a similar story with singles sales. The Beach Boys had really only broken through in Britain with "I Get Around" in 1964, but had enjoyed good singles sales since then. "Sloop John B" went to Number 2 on 21st May, just as EMI was preparing to launch *Pet Sounds*, but there was some initial uncertainty over what would be the next single. Another EMI act, Tony Rivers and the Castaways, fresh from their on-stage collaboration with Bruce, were keen to release their version of "God Only Knows," which featured extra harmony lines. The British group was told that they were to have a clear run as there were no plans to release the song as an A-side in Britain. However, just as Rivers' version was starting to gain airplay and sales in July, the decision was reversed with The Beach Boys original being issued. The U.K. release flipped the single from its current U.S. release, relegating "Wouldn't It Be Nice" to the B-side. Why no one on either side of the Atlantic saw that these two songs should have been two *separate* A-sides is difficult to understand. "God Only Knows" climbed immediately to Number 2 by the end of August, kept off the top by "Yellow Submarine." Tony Rivers and his crew were sadly cast away into the shallows of the Top 50, and missed out on what could have been their time in the sun.

Sales of Beach Boys' records in Britain during 1966 were unprecedented, and certainly benefited from Bruce Johnston's trip to these shores. They were undoubtedly the "flavour of the month," but the strength of the music itself was more responsible for this success than the clever promotion strategy. Mid-sixties British record buyers were good listeners, and for a small minority, The Beach Boys had already been hot news for three or four years. Taking Beach Boys' albums to parties during this period was decidedly unhip as the beat boom started to take hold, however feelings for the group grew steadily with boys and girls alike, and numbers like "You're So Good To Me" eventually became firm party favourites. The ground was fertile and ready, based on the great music that served as a refreshing antidote to the seemingly endless diet of Liverpool, Manchester and Birmingham acts. Only the Beatles and the Stones seemed to have the musicality to move forward at any discernible pace, so the harmonies and songs of The Beach Boys proved to be irresistible alternative fare. When the press and celebrity endorsement of *Pet Sounds* was laid at the group's door, the growth in sales was absolute. Almost overnight it was hip to talk about and like The Beach Boys.

There can be no doubt that the arrival of *Pet Sounds* had a profound effect on many musicians in Britain.

"[Lennon and McCartney] marvelled at the emotional content," Fowley remembers. "The album started the conceptual orchestrated suite albums, with the possible exception of Phil Spector's *Christmas Album*, which can maybe be seen as a slightly different case. It allowed the Beatles the luxury of taking that big orchestral step."

Keith Moon was quite clear about who was at the helm of the Beach Boys' groundbreaking new project.

"I think *Pet Sounds* illustrates the way one man's mind works," he commented at the time, "that of Brian Wilson."

Eric Clapton and his then group Cream were even more impressed.

"All of us, Ginger, Jack and I, are absolutely and completely knocked out with *Pet Sounds*," Clapton told the press. "I consider it to be one of the greatest pop LPs to ever be released. It encompasses everything that's ever knocked me out, and rolled it all into one. We're all gassed by it."

Rolling Stones manager Andrew Loog Oldham, whose Immediate Music Company handled the Beach Boys' UK Publishing, went so far as to say that, "*Pet Sounds* changed the possibilities of pop music and the potential of what could be done in the long play form."

The Beatles' producer George Martin, when interviewed by David Leaf for the *Pet Sounds Sessions* box set, was also absolute in his praise.

"The first time I heard *Pet Sounds*," Martin recalls, "I got that kind of feeling that happens less and less as one gets older and more blasé…that moment when something comes along and blows your mind. Hearing *Pet Sounds* gave me the kind of feeling that raises the hairs on the back of your neck and you say, 'What is that? It's fantastic.' It gives you an elation that is beyond logic. It's like falling in love; you're swept away by it. That's what *Pet Sounds* did to me."

Martin went on to heap fulsome praise on Brian's combinations of instruments, his thematic counterpoints and use of voices. He also acknowledged that, although certain musical progress had been made with *Rubber Soul* and *Revolver*, *Sgt. Pepper* could not have happened without Brian's masterwork. Years later, in his own television series, Martin was filmed making a pilgrimage to Brian's house and sitting with him to strip down the master tapes of "God Only Knows" to examine its components. Such comparisons of the Beatles' and The Beach Boys' work during this period is ongoing. Indeed, Bruce Johnston's own son, studying recently for his PhD in England, chose as his thesis a comparison of *Pet Sounds* and *Sgt. Pepper*. For my own part, when listening to the Beatles' work then and now, I am always aware of the conflicting directions being followed within The Beatles by Lennon and McCartney. In terms of their overall canon of songs, to have "Michelle" or "Here, There And Everywhere" to offer alongside "Tomorrow Never Knows" is of course strengthening, but at the same time confusing… However, in terms of cohesive bodies of work with their own internal logic and complete musicality, I am convinced that neither *Revolver* nor *Sgt. Pepper* can come close to *Pet Sounds*.

Much has been made of how rivalry between Brian and Lennon and McCartney spurred both on to ever greater innovations and achievements. However, The Beatles revolutionary pre-*Sgt. Pepper* album, *Revolver*, was released in the U.S. on 8th August 1966, months after the *Pet Sounds* sessions were completed. Brian was a huge fan of *Revolver*'s predecessor, *Rubber Soul*. However, in terms of musical progression, it should be remembered that the twelve-track U.S. *Rubber Soul* album only had ten tracks in common with the fourteen-track U.K. version owing to a hang-over from the earlier variations of the *Help* releases. The net result was that the U.S. version was a more introspective, acoustic-based collection, including as it did the earlier "I've Just Seen A Face" and "It's Only Love".

According to George Martin, "*Pepper* was an attempt to equal *Pet Sounds*." His use of the word *attempt* says much about Martin's view of the two albums' respective merits.

At the time, the British press began bandying around the word "genius" when discussing Wilson. It was indeed George Martin who later used the word carefully with his wealth of hindsight, "If there is one person that I

Pet Sounds *releases and sheet music.*

have to select as a living genius in pop music," Martin said in 1996, "I would choose Brian Wilson."

"I'm not a genius," Brian would say thirty years earlier, "I'm just a hard-working guy."

✱ ✱  ✱ ✱  ✱ ✱

*Pet Sounds* was to follow a strange path with Capitol Records. After the initially disappointing US sales, which soured relations between Brian and the company executives, the album was featured in press advertising alongside the hits packages.

Next, the album re-emerged as part of a "Beach Boys Deluxe Set" issued by Capitol in October 1967. This was a joint packaging of *Pet Sounds* with *Today* and *Summer Days (And Summer Nights!!)*. This opened the way for a series of re-marketed collections of earlier albums under new titles from which Capitol could extract the last drop of sales potential. Later, Beach Boys product was issued by the Brother Records (The Beach Boys' own label imprint) and Reprise association, and with the release of *Carl And The Passions*, *Pet Sounds* was re-packaged with it to make a double album. It appeared again on 13th May 1974 as a single album on Brother/Reprise, following a series of re-issues of the key tracks as singles the year before. Once again, the release was immediately followed in June 1974 by a heavily promoted Capitol hits re-package *Endless Summer*. By October the double compilation was the Number 1 album in the U.S., with a similar follow-up compilation *Spirit Of America* reaching Number 8 the next year. In Britain, the pattern of heavily-promoted hit collections mirrored the U.S., and since the mid-seventies scarcely a year has gone by without another Beach Boys re-package of a similar variety of hits.

✱ ✱  ✱ ✱  ✱ ✱

For all the commercial success of the hits collections, *Pet Sounds* has continued to grow in influence amongst music lovers, critics and musicians over the ensuing years.

**Elvis Costello:** "After the music had been dumb and goofy, and before it got too weird and spooky, there was *Pet Sounds*. So I guess that's why everyone loves it, because that's where everything was right."

**Jeff Larson**: "The album stands out to me because the innocence and beauty that Brian was able to capture with pop songs. The innocence that comes through is really a watershed for the later half of the 20th Century in terms of human communication through pop music. The beauty of melodies, harmonies, and Tony Asher's lyrics combined with the melancholy vocals by Brian and The Beach Boys are unsurpassed technically and emotionally. The music comes across as honest and revealed to the listener. So it serves as a textbook to all these things for musicians expressing themselves through the medium of popular song. It remains a testimony to youth, adulthood and probably old age since it captures what many feel and fondly look back on."

*(Jeff records for New Surf Records, along with Jeff Foskett. His albums* Watercolour Sky *(1998) and* Room For Summer *(2000) show that the legacy of the California Sound is in good hands. Find them at www.new-surf.com )*

**Andrew Gold**: "I recall *Pet Sounds* being released so vividly. I, at the tender age of 15 or something, had only been buying records for about four years, starting, not surprisingly, with The Beatles. The 60's were, for me, all about The Beatles, The Byrds, and The Beach Boys. Every record of theirs was a new sound, some new musical sophistication or some fresh approach. Being the son of a film composer, I was very into music for its own sake. New chords, new feelings, new sounds...And *PET SOUNDS* was such a huge jump up it blew me away. I was just stunned by the beauty and complexity of the music, and frankly the slightly off-kilter madness of it. It was like the music in my dreams. I still listen to it today. Brian Wilson made one of the best pop albums, if not *the* best, in history. It should be required listening for anyone with ears."

(Andrew has maintained a steady stream of great albums since his seventies hits. Specific *Pet Sounds* influences can be found on his wonderful *Greetings From Planet Love* album.)

**Dave Frishberg (Jazz Pianist):** "Peter, Paul and Mary's manager and producer gave me a copy of *Pet Sounds*, and I listened to it entranced for days. I even tried to 're-compose' the songs in an effort to imagine what Brian Wilson's creative process might feel like. I discovered that every place my instinct told me to turn right, Wilson had taken a left."

**Sean O'Hagan (The High Llamas):** "*Pet Sounds* has being lurking around in my subconscious for 20 years. When I first heard it I was confused by the mix of familiarity ("Sloop John B", "God Only Knows") and the ambition ("Let's Go Away For A While"). It was hard to grapple with the realisation that something which was part of your childhood would then form the basis of how you would relate to music for a very long time. This is what *Pet Sounds* has done to so many from my generation. We were too young to experience it first time round, but the fable and rumour soon caught up leaving us speechless and on a desperate quest to find out how this heavenly sound comes about. I can't quantify the extent to which *Pet Sounds* influenced my writing over the years but I can say that it opened up the real world of harmony and I could not imagine a world without it.

"Special mention should be made of the person who introduced the album to me 20 years ago, Cathal Coughlan [formerly of Microdisney, recently of Fatima Mansions], an act for which I will be eternally grateful."

**Todd Fletcher (June & The Exit Wounds):** "I don't have a big collection of Beach Boys albums, but you don't need it, really – it kind of all got engrained in me as I grew up, and it wasn't too hard to write songs in that style for me. I was learning jazz chords, and they all sounded familiar to me, like chords that were used in Beach Boys' songs. These are kind of tough chords, I guess, that most people don't bother to learn, so I used them as much as I could."

(June & The Exit Wounds' album "A Little More Haven" was very well received, and Todd's version of Brian's "All I Wanna Do" can be found on the Marina Records *Caroline Now* CD.)

**P.F. Sloan:** "*Pet Sounds* – I just can't listen to it – It's wonderful, quite wonderful, and I've listened to it 10,000 times. I'm not sure I can anymore… But I probably will."

(P.F.Sloan has long acknowledged a debt to Brian and The Beach Boys, whose early work he aped on his work as The Fantastic Baggies.)

**Billy Corgan (Smashing Pumpkins):** "For *Pet Sounds*, Brian Wilson turned his back on his other previous hit music. That's not genius…that's guts."

\* \* \* \* \* \*

The past two decades has seen the proliferation of polls and critics' lists of the best records of all time. Virtually every mainstream music magazine in Britain, and many more general periodicals, have come up with a list of the top 50 or top 100 albums and singles of all time. *Pet Sounds* consistently emerges near the pinnacle, and "Good Vibrations" frequently rates as the top single. In a 1993 *Sunday Times* poll of journalists and disc jockeys, *Pet Sounds*, was number 1 in the Top 100 albums (*Sgt Pepper* #2, Van Morrison's *Astral Weeks*, #3,). In 1995, the widely respected magazine *Mojo* followed suit, when its critics also voted *Pet Sounds* in their list of top albums.

Cartoonist Garry Trudeau further enhanced the status of the album when, in May 1990, he featured its CD release in a week's worth of his "Doonesbury" syndicated strip. The strip portrayed the death from AIDS of the character Andy, whose last days were lightened by having *Pet Sounds* on CD, with the final message on his pad simply being "Brian Wilson is God".

# Interlude

*My requests for submissions for this book brought out not only the wonderful musical comments and testimonials found elsewhere in the main text, but also what I can only describe as honest and emotional responses that were too beautiful to leave out. Below are some quotations about the feelings evoked by Brian Wilson's music.*

"I had my sleep disturbed by a nightmare, one that I have since found is all too familiar with parents. In the dream I was made aware of the death of my eight-year-old daughter, Amanda, and I was powerless to do anything but weep uncontrollably. Needless to say, this jolted me to consciousness – it was just past 3:00 AM – where I found myself shaking, near tears. So, I did what any sane person would do in such a situation, at such a time: I got up, found my stereo bootleg of *Pet Sounds* (which I keep beneath my pillow), put it on, and listened, peacefully…"

– Neal Umphred

(Neal is a well known music writer, and this excerpt is taken from the end of his "Let's Go Away For Awhile" article in the *Back To The Beach* reader, Helter Skelter, 1997)

"It was only when I reached my early to mid-twenties, that its power and overwhelming beauty took hold on my psyche. It was quite a humbling experience learning to play "I Just Wasn't Made For These Times;" it's amazing how something seemingly so simple could prove to be so intricate. The way that "God Only Knows" reaches out on so many levels, but still manages to hit you straight in the heart is just further testimony to Brian Wilson's genius. *Pet Sounds* is a complete sensory experience and to introduce someone new to its beauty is surely one of the greatest gifts that you could ever make."

–Robin Wills

(Robin was the songwriter/ guitarist with UK's powerpop-surf-jangle merchants The Barracudas, and now he is a consultant, living happily with two Goldfish, a Golden Retriever and his soulmate Nicola.)

"When I'm an old, old man looking back over his scrapbook of memories one of the key chapters is definitely going to be *Pet Sounds* and the great joy it has always given to me. And to so many others! It is an album which age doesn't wither, which grows ever richer with time like the finest wine or the most loving relationship between two dear friends."

– Sid Griffin (Former Long Ryder Sid Griffin is the leader of psychedelic alt-country exponents Western Electric, a writer for many publications and a Beach Boys fan since Valentine's Day 1964 when his Mom bought him the *Surfer Girl* album as a present instead of candy.)

"First impressions of *Pet Sounds* are probably somehow visual ones, wrapped up in childhood memories of staring with wonder at the album's cover. For my brother and me, our parents' LP collections doubled as our favorite toys. On the *Pet Sounds'* sleeve, The Beach Boys seemed to lead me into their own imaginative world, rather than posing for a calculated photo shoot atop a shiny car or across a waxed down surfboard... I felt like I was observing a private, genuinely innocent moment, one The Beach Boys created on their own terms."

– Jennifer Baron

(Jennifer writes and records with The Ladybug Transistor, whose albums are delightful soundscapes of summer fun.)

"Jimmy Bumer's dad owned a candy shop. One day a year, a few of the kids on the street would be lucky enough to earn a free 'shop' at the store, filling their bags to the brim with bars, pops, drops and fizzes. Jimmy and I, being best friends, would leave together, glorified by our loot. Where would we go? Our rendezvous point was none other than Jimmy's bunk bed, our candy flagship, and there we'd sit, surveying our treasure. From the top bunk we'd look over the waves into a giant mirror, as we began our long descent into confectionery heaven, guided along by our special own master of ceremonies, Brian Wilson. As *Pet Sounds* roared over the deck we chomped and chewed and thought how 'nice' it would be when we were older. Staring curiously at ourselves, Brian's orchestral masterpiece told us about a life to come and hinted that growing older might not be that bad."

– Jeff Baron

(Jeff also writes and records with The Ladybug Transistor and The Essex Green.) "[*In response to Brian's 1966 comment, "I'm not a genius, I'm just a hardworking guy,"*] Well, how about instinctive, extraordinary, imaginative, creative and inventive?"

– Marc Carroll

(Marc is a singer/songwriter who has recorded with The Hormones. His song, "Mr Wilson" can be found on their album *Where Old Ghosts Meet* [V2]).

"*Pet Sounds* is one of the most musically profound albums ever made, but for me what really makes it special is the purity of spirit throughout it. Picasso talked about being able to draw like the most accomplished adult by the age of 14, then spending the rest of his life trying to be able to draw like a child again. Brian Wilson never lost that purity, innocence and truth that most of us long to reclaim. *Pet Sounds* is one of those special works that inspire an evangelical impulse in those who love it. I've definitely spent more of my life and energy promoting it than any of the records I've made myself. I know I'm not unique in this. It has not only enriched my life as an artist but helped me in my personal life. I was going through a very bad time a number of years ago and when things just got too much I'd lie down and listen to *Pet Sounds*. By the end of it the world would seem a lot better again. It's the sonic equivalent of a frightened child being comforted in its loving mother's arms."

– Douglas T. Stewart

(Douglas recorded with the BMX Bandits for many years, and is often involved in Brian Wilson/Beach Boys events in the media and at fan conventions)

"My parents had an original *Pet Sounds* mono copy and I played it into the ground. I began learning all of the vocal parts, the horn parts, the strings, everything. Here I began to understand the craft and sophistication that pop music could possess. "So now I have been listening to *Pet Sounds* for nearly 25 years. Nothing ever changes in these listenings. Brian and the boys still make me cry every time. Brian always makes me feel like I make baby music. Brian makes nearly everything else before or since sound slightly stupid. Listening to *Pet Sounds* hurts… Not even the Beatles were able to put together a whole work with such singular force. I am sure that Paul would agree with this. Because of *Pet Sounds* all of us in the musical creative community have the life long assignment of spinning our wheels with no hope of ever getting to the level of heaven that Brian was residing in. No matter how it was born, it was. And now it lives forever as a monument to God, a beacon of what man cannot be. It is blameless."

– Eric Matthews

(Eric's version of "Lonely Sea" can be found on the compilation "Caroline Now" on Marina Records. His albums include *It's Heavy In Here* and *The Lateness Of The Hour.*)

"I always make best friends in the most roundabout of ways, it seems, and my discovery of *Pet Sounds* was certainly no exception. I still find myself slipping the latest version of Brian's 'little album that could' reassuringly into back pockets whenever people I know have in any way lost touch, perhaps lost loved ones, or have simply just lost their way. I mean, what are best friends for?"          – Gary Pig Gold

(Gary Pig Gold is now based in New Jersey USA, where he merrily writes about, performs, produces and releases music on a very near daily basis. He can be contacted at PIGPROD@aol.com)

"I kept reading that *Pet Sounds* was a big influence on artists, and decided to pick up a used copy on vinyl and see for myself what all the fuss was about. As soon as I put it on, I felt like I was listening to the musical version of the Bible! Everything I loved about music seemed to be contained in these 13 songs: perfect melodies, lush arrangements, dense harmonies, and 'fantasy-land' instrumentation. It seemed like all the bands I was into were using this as their blueprint. But even more than just great musicianship, production, and songwriting, there was such *emotion*."

– Linus of Hollywood

(Linus Of Hollywood has recently released an album full of Brianesque harmonies and melodies called *Your Favorite Record* on his own Franklin Castle label.)

"Brian Wilson was a gifted cook: he put together a menu which none has ever tried to re-create. Like apple and cinnamon, ham and mustard, lamb and mint – these are sounds which *belong* together uniquely, perfectly. The resulting dishes are as pure as the individual ingredients that created them. *Pet Sounds* is the banquet he prepared, still as delicious and as fresh as when he dished it up. And there is no recipe book."                – Sean Macreavy

(Sean is an active musician and songwriter, whose 1994 album *Dumb Angel*, on Japan's M&M Records, includes his vocal version of "Let's Go Away For Awhile".)


"As to me, I can only say that I love it as the sun, or as the ocean. Unquestionably, but with a sense of the miraculous. As something monumental, incandescent, finding renewal within itself – yet familiar, not one of those mega-works which, in effect, belittle the listener. What else could I say? That this record had saved my life when I was trying to get over a disastrous love affair? I'll stop here. You probably have your own *Pet Sounds* salvation story. I'm just one of the family, as you are."

Louis Philippe

(Louis is a well known European musician whose *Ivory Tower* album features a splendid cover of "Guess I'm Dumb".)

## Chapter 7
## EVERYTHING I KNOW: TRIALS AND TRIBULATIONS

*"When we finally heard 'Good Vibrations' edited and mixed, we thought we were going to have the biggest hit in the world or the career was over."*
– Bruce Johnston

*"We got a little arty about it...We had a lot of problems...We got really stoned...never finished...We didn't have any energy...lyrics were so poetic and symbolic they were abstract...tracks that weren't made for vocals."*
– Brian Wilson (A selection of quotes about the post-*Pet Sounds* period)

"Good Vibrations" was released in November 1966. It was universally rapturously received as a new advance in pop artistry, and became a huge worldwide hit. However, while the single's success saw Brian at the zenith of his popularity, it also marked the beginning of a rapid turnaround in his fortunes.

"Good Vibrations" was originally begun with Tony Asher as part of the *Pet Sounds* writing sessions. Having rejected it for inclusion in its original form for that album, Brian planned to spend more time on it after the *Pet Sounds* release. He proceeded to experiment with different feels and arrangements for some 90 hours of tape, in four different studios, before finally constructing a finished master from many separate, quite disparate fragments. Ex-Sunray Rick Henn remembers, "I was in the studio and saw the actual tape for the finished version. I've never seen one like it! It was so cut and pasted. There must have been between 50 and 60 edits visible on it!" Despite the edited sections of the end product, the world received it with open arms – though some pop fans apparently found its switches of tempo made it unsatisfactory dancing material – and the story of its recording was central to everything written about it. For the first time the making of a hit was bigger news than the group itself, and Brian took the full glare of the spotlight. Kim Fowley felt this had an extreme effect on Brian.

"The Beatles/Beach Boys rivalry had been fun," says Fowley, "but now he was being compared to other composers, and he also had to compete with himself. He was to suffer from Leonard Bernstein's anointing, and quite possibly suffered from resentment from other Beach Boys, who maybe thought they weren't getting enough attention as he got all the glory. Was it right for him to be singled out? Remember, Brian was *all alone* as a 'genius' – Lennon and McCartney had each other, George Martin, and Brian Epstein. He had added a new burden of having to struggle harder to top himself."

Brian immersed himself in trying to come up with something more breathtaking and innovative than either *Pet Sounds* or "Good Vibrations." This involved him adopting Van Dyke Parks as his new lyrical collaborator and embarking on what Parks would call an "American Gothic Trip." This was the album now known as "the legendary unreleased *Smile* album."

"Van Dyke dragged Brian away from the familiar territory of romantic love towards a new style of writing," writer Peter Doggett observed, "full of elliptical imagery and verbal free associations... On previous albums, Brian Wilson had conceived each song as a separate entity. With *Smile*, all boundaries were knocked aside, and he crafted fragmentary pieces of music, some conventional, others totally oddball, which he tried to shape into some kind of coherent whole."

In the context of the musical growth up to and including this album, the new sounds and "songs" – or song fragments – bear little resemblance to the feel of Brian's emotionally maturing music. What we have instead is a dream play of brooding, conflicting musical ideas.

No doubt Brian's increased drug use during the period caused the thematic threads to fall apart. The song "Cabinessence" – later released on *20/20* – may be a good encapsulation of what *Smile* could have been. Within this multi-faceted song is the embryo of a musical history of American culture. In the Brian Wilson documentary *A Beach Boy's Tale* (A&E Television 1999), former Smashing Pumpkin Billy Corgan saw *Smile* as Brian "trying to take Mark Twain into rock 'n' roll." "Cabinessence" depicts images of the railroad, migration and wide-open spaces – visions which could have been brought to the rest of the album. Dominic Priore, in his *Look! Listen! Vibrate! Smile!* scrapbook (Last Gasp, 1995), picks up this Americana theme as being partially rooted in Van Dyke's knowledge of American history and folklore, and potentially likely to have formed at least half of the album. It was a rich resource area that Brian and Van Dyke were to return to in some respects with their nineties collaboration, *Orange Crate Art*. *Smile* could have been the history of the American Dream, which Brian's upbringing in Hawthorne symbolised. Later strands of the work, such as the elemental suite of songs on side two of *Smile*, could have formed a totally separate project.

The chronology of this period is interesting. Writers often refer to *Pet Sounds* and *Smile* as two very different albums (which they were) from two different times (which they were not). Most observers place the recording sessions about six months apart. This is simply not true. As Bruce Johnston confirms, there was no break between the *Pet Sounds* sessions and the writing of *Smile*. Furthermore, there was recording overlap.* Nonetheless, Brian was clearly pushing the envelope further as each session followed on from the previous one, with all the praise and pressure – exacerbated by Capitol's increasingly impatient demands for product – pushing him ever further onwards and further out there.

As time went on, it became increasingly unlikely that Brian would ever be able to assemble the myriad disparate fragments of his new project with anything like the cohesion and success of "Good Vibrations."

"Heroes and Villains," Brian's hugely ambitious follow-up to "Good Vibrations," was finally released in a truncated version in July 1967. Fascinating, if nothing like as catchy as its predecessor, the single met a less-than enthusiastic U.S. reception. By now The Beatles' attempt to equal *Pet Sounds*, *Sgt Pepper*'s *Lonely Hearts Club Band* had been out a good two months and instantly eclipsed its inspiration. Post-*Pepper*, the musical world would never be the same again. "Heroes and Villains" was followed in September 1967 by *Smiley Smile*, a watered down, unfocused but strangely compelling collection that included some of the *Smile* material. Depressed at what he perceived as rejection of his efforts, hindered by drug abuse and marital difficulties, Brian lost the plot, musical and otherwise, and went into a period of steady physical and mental decline. While Brian was somewhat active in the last years of the decade, his work rate was a fraction of what it had been.

The Beach Boys continued recording and touring, with Carl and Dennis doing their best to plug the gaps caused by their elder brother removing himself from writing, recording and production. The following sixties original albums (*Smiley Smile*, *Wild Honey*, *Friends* and *20/20*) were all good and interesting albums, but it was evident that there was not a consistent captain at the helm. In place of full and adventurous orchestral productions, there was a mixture of styles, whimsy and even a return on occasions to filler tracks. Other members of the group were filling the songwriting vaccuum caused by Brian's increasing withdrawal, but it was not until *Sunflower*, released in 1970, that the Beach Boys came up with an album that represented an important and cohesive body of work. Ironically, this record was not the product of one mind, but the flowering of the individual talents within the band which was to keep the ship afloat for the

---

* An example of this is the recording of "Cabinessence", the vocals of which were tackled even before *Pet Sounds'* release. Bruce Johnston sang them over the phone to me on his British promo trip, and described the recent session.

coming decade. It was on *Sunflower*, for instance, that Dennis really emerged as a major force, both as a singer and a writer, especially with the lovely "Forever" which was to set the tone for his musical development. Bruce contributed the still under-rated "Tears In The Morning", which hits many of the emotional buttons that were so evident on *Pet Sounds*. Al was co-writer of both "At My Window" and the delicate "Our Sweet Love", with even Carl taking a co-credit on the latter. The singing on this album was probably amongst the best the group ever managed, especially on "Add Some Music To Your Day". The album saw the other Beach Boys come of age just as Brian's first period of major withdrawal became complete. A second major period of Beach Boys' achievement was upon them that was to gather a new generation of fans, and lead to the seventies albums, *Surf's Up* and *Holland*.

After Brian's 1972 partial-involvement with the *American Spring* album, which he cut at home with his wife Marilyn and sister-in-law Diane, there followed a lengthy period of minimal creativity. Brian would struggle to complete any cohesive work until he wrote and recorded *The Beach Boys Love You* in 1977. Sadly, this album had none of the adventurous instrumentation of *Pet Sounds*.

In the seventies and eighties, Brian spent two long spells of time in the care of Dr. Eugene Landy, who was asked by the family and group to clean up the downward-spiralling Brian and try to return him to reasonable health. The first period was when Brian was still married to Marilyn; the second was after their split.

Brian's marriage to Marilyn failed in September 1978 and they divorced early the next year. In his Landy-supervised 1991 "autobiography", *Wouldn't It Be Nice*, Brian admits to various incidences of sexual experimentation that were detrimental to his marriage. It is reasonable to assume that elements of his crisis originated in his drug-fuelled friendships of the late sixties and seventies. All these problems conspired to remove the emotional base from which Brian could grow musically. Officially diagnosed as a paranoid schizophrenic and a manic-depressive, Brian felt "depressed and lost" after divorcing Marilyn.

The Landy years are remembered for the gradual insinuation of the doctor into more and more of Brian's business and musical affairs. This was justifiable up to a point, in that musical activity was a reasonable way to pull Brian back into a more active lifestyle. It is also very probable that Dr. Landy actually saved Brian's life by pulling him away from drug and junkfood excesses and lethargic torpor, but along the way a line was overstepped and the Doctor-patient relationship became counter-productive. Brian was still recovering in the late eighties when he cut his first official solo album. Brian's earlier attempt to collaborate with his old friend Gary Usher had foundered when Landy steered his patient away from what the doctor perceived to be a disruptive relationship. It is probable that, had that work continued, a good album would have resulted. Usher kept daily diaries of the events, collected by historian Stephen McParland in *The Wilson Project* book, which illustrate his growing frustration with Landy's increasing interference and Brian's inability to function without him.

With Usher out of the way, Andy Paley was brought in to help with the solo album.

"I was brought into the picture by Lenny Waronker and Seymour Stein of Sire Records," Paley explains. "Seymour had a Brian solo album idea, and he had heard some of my songs. I was in London and he called me from a Rock & Roll Hall of Fame dinner where he was sitting with Brian. Well, Brian wasn't talking to anyone, and Seymour wanted some ideas for involving him in conversation. I suggested talking about some of the obscurer songs, like 'Solar System,' and apparently that sparked some conversation. Anyway, they decided to bring me over, and I moved to L.A. to work with Brian. I had no relationship with Landy, but he was around and was a force that had to be reckoned with."

Progress was initially awkward, but Paley ended up as co-writer/producer on some of the album's strongest tracks.

"There were an awful lot of cooks!" says Paley. "People expected a lot, which was really unfair on Brian. What you achieve at 20 doesn't really happen again – well, maybe you can be as strong, but not as much... not as often. You don't feel the drive in the same way, and not everybody involved with that album was sensitive to that. Once in a while Brian would do something great, but it was difficult for other people to leave it untainted. I tried to work with just the two of us, and from that 'Rio Grande' and 'Meet Me In My Dreams Tonight' emerged as pretty organic pieces. Brian was fine when left to his own devices."

Even with Gary Usher out of the picture, the album that emerged in 1988 was generally considered to be a fine effort, despite its plethora of mysterious, and controversial, Landy co-writing credits. Intriguingly, the eponymously-titled album included an interesting suite called "Rio Grande," which would have been ideal fare for the unrealized Americana theme on *Smile*.

The warm reception for Brian's solo album showed the world that, with help, he could come up with accessible new music. This contributed to a gradual rebuilding of his lost confidence. His plea for "Love And Mercy" on that album's best-known track was a graphic encapsulation of his state of mind at the time, and has since assumed great stature in the Wilson canon,

*The 1988 solo album.*

taking on a new level of poignancy with the tragic newscasts of September 11th 2001.

> *"I was lyin' in my room and the news came on TV*
> *A lotta people out there hurtin' and it really scares me*
> *Love and mercy, that's what you need tonight*
> *So, Love and mercy to you and your friends tonight."*

A few years later, the publication of *Wouldn't It Be Nice*, gave rise to a brief meeting between Brian and his *Pet Sounds* collaborator, Tony Asher. After minimal and intermittent contact over the years, Asher attended a signing for the ghost-written book.

"He barely recognised me," Asher sadly recalls. "He just signed the book, robot-like, 'To you and the family.'" More recent contact between the pair has been more positive, and in the later nineties, a joint-writing session produced new songs, including the lovely "Everything I Need." This song has been recorded both by Brian's two daughters Carnie and Wendy as The Wilsons, and by Jeff Foskett on his *Twelve By Twelve* album, with Brian contributing vocally to both versions. Asher speaks warmly of all his recent meetings with Brian, especially time spent at Brian's home, where Asher reports that he is considerably more relaxed and interactive than at public venues.

The Brian of the nineties was a wiser man, surrounding himself with more benign helpers and friends. He remarried, to Melinda, with whom he adopted two baby girls, and his relationship with his daughters Carnie and

Wendy also improved. His own solo work continued with sympathetic producers like Andy Paley, Don Was and Joe Thomas. There was also a well-received collaboration with *Smile*-sparring partner Van Dyke Parks, in which Brian provided lead and background vocals for Parks' *Orange Crate Art* album.

Hardcore fans and writers argue endlessly as to the relative worth of Brian's recent projects; the essential fact is that his active return to music was an enormous step forward.

*The Don Was produced album.*

# Chapter 8
# GRADUALLY RE-EMERGING: BRIAN IN THE NINETIES

*One of the many* Sweet Insanity *bootlegs.*

*"It was me with the concepts and Brian with the music, and that's where the strength lay. 'Kokomo' was a No 1 hit in 1988, whereas Brian's solo album came out and didn't have one hit record on it...Who wants to buy an album [*Sweet Insanity*] and hear a load of songs about therapy and mental illness? I don't think that's very mainstream pop."* – Mike Love, 1993

*"I just want to motivate people to hear good music. To play it, to feel it and say, 'Right on, that's it!' I know I've been through a hell of a lot in my life, but I'm still around and feel I can do more."* – Brian Wilson, 1998

Brian began the nineties working on a second solo album, *Sweet Insanity*. This totally Landy-driven album was recorded but was generally seen as weak fare, dogged by psychobabble lyrics and a poor production. It remains unissued, although it was widely circulated in bootleg form on the fan circuit. Andy Paley was again involved, "I played and sang on that album. It was a Landy record. He'd just tell Brian what to do, so it's a lot less than a true Brian Wilson record. None of it was Brian's idea, though I think 'Rainbow Eyes' is a pretty song."

In 1995, Brian took part in a joint album/film project with British producer Don Was. The musical content was made up of eleven remakes of previous Brian songs, including a maturer and more reflective "Caroline No." Was pointed to Brian's vocal as the prime example of why he wanted to make the accompanying film, "My personal favourite is 'Caroline No,' his paean to lost innocence. I hear the weary voice of a man who's been hurled through the emotional ringer and yet, one can plainly discern the youthful sweetness, optimism and goodness that characterises Brian's soul."

The remake of "Do It Again" included back-up vocals from Carnie and Wendy Wilson, who repaid their dad for his backgrounds on their own earlier "Wilsons" album. Despite all the crafted care, the album did not spark much sales interest, probably because it didn't go into new territory.

1998 saw the release of the Joe Thomas-produced *Imagination* album, which had a bright and lively feel from collaboration with other musicians. Brian's singing, for those who knew it well, was lighter and more youthful than may have been reasonably expected, but even with the electronic wizardry that made this possible the whole album was a great improvement on the more recent attempts. This mixture of new songs, ballads and a couple of revivals ("Let Him Run Wild" and "Keep An Eye On Summer"), obviously pleased Brian himself. "It was recorded in the Mid-West," he enthused. "I love recording in that studio. It has safe and productive vibrations. The vibe is so critical to me."

In the mid-nineties, when the Californian Conservancy Board finally

*The promo cover for the* Imagination *album.*

prohibited Landy from making further contact with Brian, Brian called Andy Paley, "The day after the Board made their decision, Brian called up and said 'I'm free! I can do what I like now!' He came over the day after that and we did 'I'm Broke,' a song which he had written by himself."

Brian and Paley have frequently worked together ever since, and have produced a welter of still-unreleased tracks. Paley describes a wider and more co-operative collaboration than those of Brian's other co-writers:

"When we wrote, Brian would often do the lyrics. Some songs, like 'You're Still A Mystery,' were really 50/50 – music and lyrics – but with one like 'Getting In Over My Head,' Brian wrote the whole bridge and some lyrics to my music. Each song had its own story. One particular one was with 'Soul Searchin.' I was in London producing, and Brian wanted to work on it, so he went out and actually bought the travel tickets for him and Melinda himself. He arranged it all himself, and came to London and and said 'Let's go to Paris and see the Mona Lisa!'"

Paley maintains regular contact with Brian, and one of their most recent joint efforts involved cutting a signature surf-rock tune for Rodney Bingenheimer's famous KROQ radio show "Rodney On The Roq," featuring vocals from Andy, his brother Jonathan, Jeff Foskett and Brian. The whole thing was enjoyed by all, and most importantly for Brian perhaps, was on the radio two days after its completion!

Another point of involvement for Paley was in supplying a live back-up band at various points for Brian:

"I did a bunch of gigs with him way back in 1988 for the first solo album. We did a few with The Beach Boys. Then we did some more when Don Was was making his movie about Brian. We had a great little band that included Elliot Easton (Ex-Cars) and Billy West and we even had a string quartet. We played L.A., Chicago and the Sundance Film Festival. At one date at Santa Monica, a Brian tribute concert that Rodney [Bingenheimer] had helped organise, we opened with 'Shut Down Part 2,' which surprised quite a few people! That was where Rodney introduced Brian to The Wondermints, who were also on the bill."

This introduction would prove to be of particular importance, as it led directly to full live tours. However, before the live work there were some other important developments. The emergence of CDs in the eighties had a profound impact on Brian's career. Record companies soon recognised that the length and quality possible with the new format meant reissues not previously thought possible were now extremely viable. By the eighties and nineties, Capitol Records had become a completely different record label, and its executives were now happy to consider extensive and intelligent remarketing of The Beach Boys' catalogue. In 1990, Capitol issued the famed 'twofers' – pairs of Beach Boys albums placed on single discs. In addition, each CD had relevant outtakes tagged on. The issues were extremely well packaged, with extensive notes from Beach Boys writer David Leaf, and often contained notes from Brian as well. The success and acclaim made Capitol consider a full, retrospective Box Set, which arrived on four discs in 1993. The care lavished on the selection and presentation of the catalogue was unprecedented, and it received a mass of plaudits from all quarters and generated strong sales.

Capitol had always treated *Pet Sounds* separately. It was the one album not released in the 'twofer' format, and it remained on catalogue as a stand-alone album. The intervening years since its original 1966 issue had seen its reputation grow beyond hardcore fans and musicians, and by the 1990's, *Pet Sounds* was universally accepted as one of the most influential albums of all time. Legendary figures such as Paul McCartney, Elton John and George Martin repeatedly acknowledged its brilliance. Musicians of the next two generations, including R.E.M., Oasis, Tears For Fears and Sonic Youth, were also vocal about its power and beauty. In the early nineties, Capitol began to take notice of such polls and opinions, and also realised that a true stereo version had never been released.

# Chapter 9
## THE SUM OF THE PARTS:
## THE PET SOUNDS SESSIONS BOX SET

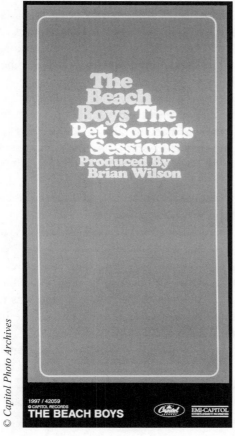

*© Capitol Photo Archives*

*"What is apparent from the Sessions box set is the extraordinary complexity of the backing tracks, much of which was lost in the final mix as the vocals often mask these intricacies. Thank goodness we are privileged to hear that work in isolation, proof, as if it was needed, of Brian's imaginative scoring and his command of his favourite instrument, a studio full of musicians."*
– Chris White (British harmony singer/songwriter)

*"As a contemporary musician you don't really have an 'education' proper, but you could do worse than listen to the* Pet Sounds *box set and hear Brian at his peak, creating music, being nice and making everybody laugh. You might be making your own records in the shadow of such scary greatness but you can still be inspired by his tunes, his spirit and his bravery."*

– David Scott (Pearlfishers)

Retrospective projects by younger executives of large corporations often fail to capture the feel and charm of the originals (witness the *Back To The Beach* film that attempted to re-create the innocence of the sixties beach movies). With the *Sessions* set, Capitol made two crucial decisions early on in their engagement of engineer Mark Linett and writer David Leaf, who were perhaps the only people who could deliver a product worthy of the album and Brian's work. Both had previously worked on the twofers and the retrospective box set.

In the early nineties, with the marketing opportunity of a *Pet Sounds* thirty-year anniversary, Capitol got serious about producing a release that would appeal to both serious musicologists and hardcore fans. The first key activity was to examine the tape library, and make some sort of decision as to the extent of the session tapes to be used. Brian was consulted early on in the process to judge whether a stereo version was acceptable to him, and to introduce the idea of separating the vocal and instrumental tracks as had proved so popular on the earlier retrospective box set. Brian was interested in all these aspects of the project, and work continued toward a four-CD set with a remastered mono version of the album at the end. Whilst David Leaf set about the huge task of contacting and interviewing everyone involved with the original album, Mark Linett worked towards constructing the first-ever stereo version of the LP.* Mark's strong notion was not to attempt to improve upon the mono *Pet Sounds*, but rather to enhance listening pleasure by providing a different version.

Linett's first job was to gather the multi-track masters from which the original mono master mix was made. It was evident that certain changes in final mono mix stage were not reflected by the multi-tracks. Linett had most difficulty with "Wouldn't It Be Nice," which turned out to be an edited

---

* In 1966, the album was issued by Capitol in mono and 'Duophonic', which was a special electronic re-processing technique. It referred to bass and treble separation, and use of a 'doubler,' which meant that a mono track could be split onto two channels, and played together with a very slight delay applied to one of them. The results supposedly enhanced the sound as everything appeared to have a good deal of echo. In a *Goldmine* magazine interview in 1980, Chuck Britz referred to this as Capitol's "kind of pseudo-stereo that they used to use."

amalgam of the multi-track mix. Assembling a stereo mix with instrumental values that satisfied Brian was enormously challenging. In most cases the musicians were split on to three tracks with horns on one, basses and guitars on another, and the basic rhythm track on the third. The tracks were weighted differently this way, making it tricky to construct a balanced, satisfying stereo mix. Brian's habit of dubbing down from one four-track to another also led to second or third generations of tape and associated problems.

Noise reduction systems had been employed on the 'twofer' sets, but with improved EQ facilities Linett chose not to use any such devices on this project. Linett's view of his job was to capture the essence of Brian's 1966 achievements, "They're great songs and everything, but the uniqueness about them is in partly how he used those instruments to get those sounds, and partly the vocals. That's what makes those records so exceptional."

There were some parts where the vocals-only tracks could be 'unlocked,' as with the vocal lines behind the chorus of "I Wasn't Made For These Times." These ran to three different layers, including one sung in Spanish, behind the "*Sometimes I feel very sad…*" line. Various snippets, including this Spanish section, are included as hidden tracks on the *Sessions* box set, so patience is required when listening to the end tracks on three of the discs! "Wouldn't It Be Nice" was unpacked in different stages: the purely instrumental track first, the vocals with the lead second, and finally the backgrounds without the lead. When listening to this track it is possible to get an idea of why this was the most difficult song from the group-vocal standpoint. Linett carefully used technology to reconstruct certain vocal tracks that lacked doubled leads on the multi-track masters (Brian sometimes doubled a vocal at the final mono mix down stage). Linett's challenge was to get the vocals in perfect sync with the original instrumental multi-tracks by transferring the instrumentals to a new digital multi-track machine and then manually synchronising the vocals using an original 1966 dub as a guide. After consultation with Brian, Linett decided to mix out the background studio chatter in the stereo mix in order to make it clearer.

"Brian wasn't involved day-to-day in the studio," explains Linett, "as there was no real need for that. I would do mixes, take them to his house, and he would make comments. When he was satisfied, then that was it for a track. At times we were going back for up to three generations, but even so we were able to make the stereo close to the original mono… Mono deals with the depth of instruments – front to back. The tapes we had – and we had around 99 percent of them – allowed for a nice stereo mix. Brian can hear the results of a stereo mix."

The results of Linett's work make the *Sessions* box set a superb purchase for anyone who seeks to go further than the original mono album. However, there is no doubt that the original form of the album stands up well. When questioned by Sean Lennon in 1999 as to whether or not *Pet Sounds* would have been better with modern digital mixing, Brian replied, "It might not have been so good, believe it or not. Because in the room, the room was so filled with good vibes that, you know, even a four-track was okay in those days. It was fine!" In 1999, Capitol also released a single CD that included the mono album, the stereo version, and "Hang On To Your Ego," (the original form of "I Know There's An Answer"). A separate stereo CD issue has never been part of Capitol's plans.

David Leaf's construction of the box set booklets is immaculate. The first, 36-page book serves as an introductory programme featuring the history, technical and musician credits and lyrics. It also features visual material and a new message from Brian himself. Reflecting on the position the record has attained in people's affections, he says humbly:

"When people come up to me and tell me it's their favourite album, I feel honoured. I also think people are pulling my leg when they tell me it's the greatest thing ever written...It's just a matter of realising that the songs we did in 1966 are very much alive in 1996. And to be aware of the love in those songs that is able to give the listener the feeling of being loved, which is something we kinda like to do. We like to give our love."

The second booklet is named "The Making Of *Pet Sounds*," and includes interviews with all the people that contributed directly the album. The release, when it finally appeared, was prefaced in this booklet by a short piece from Mike Love, the main purpose of which appeared to be to stress the album as part of the whole ongoing Beach Boys' canon of work.

The release of the set gathered a great deal of positive publicity, although some well-known writers, including *Record Collector*'s Peter Doggett, saw it as appealing mainly to hard core fans and music writers and insiders. Whilst this is true to an extent, the set is ordered and selected to allow appeal for a larger market. Doggett saw the stereo mix as an "intriguing experiment...that might actually make it more accessible to a modern audience." This is true, but the compilers of the set knew the stereo version could send new listeners back to pick up on the original mono. Moreover, the project contributed further to the original *Pet Sounds* album's classic status.

✴ ✴  ✴ ✴ ✴

The arrival of the *Sessions* Box set was long delayed from its original announcement. It was not long before rumours were spreading that it was discontent within the Beach Boys camp that was causing the delay.

Furthermore, it did not take much guessing to put Mike Love central to any dissent. As discussed in previous chapters, Love had not always been present at the original *Pet Sounds* sessions, and he is well known to have expressed disquiet at the lyrical content and the radical step away from known and trusted Beach Boys' fare. However, as the album gathered ever growing critical and customer support, Love's position seemed to subtly shift. In his lyrically nostalgic seventies song "Brian's Back", he reverentially refers to "ole *Pet Sounds*", and in some interviews he was happy to be one of several who claim to have come up with the album title. This trend went against the background of the album's tracks being generally discarded from seventies and eighties Beach Boys sets lists (aside from the obvious hits). It should also be remembered that "Wouldn't It Be Nice", one of the consistently most popular *Pet Sounds* numbers around the world, was one of the songs that Mike subsequently claimed a co-writing credit for.

When the *Sessions* set finally arrived, it was not surprising that the "Making of..." booklet began with a statement of full involvement from Mike. However this move is interpreted, it should be remembered that Mike has never made any secret of his desire to work with the ultimately commercial catalogue. If he is now seeking to ally himself more closely with the album he is really only doing what virtually everyone else did – taking a little while to adjust to the magnificence of Brian's new music. It just took Mike a little longer than the rest of the world!

*The U.S. tour poster.*

In 2000, Brian decided to tour *Pet Sounds* as a fully-orchestrated live event. Just ten years before this, the idea of Brian undertaking a tour would have been absurd. Perhaps the key as to why it finally happened is best expressed by touring musician Jeff Foskett, who says, "He's doing it because he doesn't have to."

Prior to the album tour, Brian assembled musicians who could accompany him sympathetically on the sort of show that he sought to present. Encouraged by his wife Melinda to try to do a show that would match the high esteem that people held him in, Brian took steps to work toward his first full solo concerts as opposed to the shorter sets he had previously intermittently performed. Beginning near his then-summer home in Chicago in 1998, he assembled two forty-minute sets with an eleven-piece band which included The Wondermints and Jeff Foskett, who had played with The Beach Boys' touring band in the 1980s, as well as some top-notch session musicians. With sets that mixed songs from the *Imagination* album with some from *Pet Sounds*, Brian emerged slightly taken aback but triumphant.

"In the beginning it was everybody's concern whether he could handle the road," says The Wondermints' Darian Sahanaja. "We started out real easy with a short four-show run and were surprised by how well he'd taken to it. We took on more and more shows, and by the end of the tour leg we would notice him just starting to get going. 'Onward and upward!' was what he would say, and that's when I knew he could handle anything."

"When I was in The Beach Boys in the 1980's," Jeff Foskett reflects, "We had our own jet, stayed in only the nicest Five Star accommodations, made

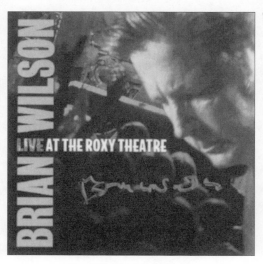

*The 2000 double live CD.*

*Brian straps on the bass for the encores. Photo: Robert Mattau*

more money per show than ever… but all those things have a price. The price was the band became complacent and downright tired. We were touring 180 days a year; the music suffered greatly. Carl knew it and tried to change things but ultimately gave in to the heavy touring schedule. The Brian Wilson band is much different. As a band we rehearse often; we offer one another encouragement and helpful, constructive suggestions. We hold a Spirit Circle before each performance, which to me is a big part of the success of the show. We honour God, the Creator, the Great Spirit, whatever one wants to call Him when we perform. That makes a huge difference. We are not performing to be recognised, rather to make the music sound as good as it possibly can and let Brian be recognised for the achievements and accomplishments that he has made in his life. It's about Brian and the music – not about personal ego."

The unit gelled wonderfully, and the results are best captured on the 2000 double-CD release of *Brian Wilson – Live At The Roxy Theatre*. Recorded over two nights, it captures the intimacy and enjoyment and Brian's voice is as good as could be expected. As he introduces the first encore "Caroline No," he chuckles and refers to it as a "sweet girlie tune," then proceeds to sing what are possibly the highest notes he has hit in years.

From the success of this first tour, which included excellent versions of two *Pet Sounds* songs, plans were to tour the whole album, with the band augmented by a live orchestra.

"It is somewhat common knowledge that [Brian] didn't come up with the idea initially," says Darian. "Given the heightened awareness for the album with the anniversary and general artistic acknowledgement in recent years, it was a reasonable suggestion to make. Brian was lukewarm to the idea at first simply because he didn't think it could be pulled off. I believe his mind has been changed!"

*Brian on the tour, taking the plaudits. Photo: Robert Mattau*

Once Brian warmed to the idea, he firmly grasped the reins.

"Brian oversaw everything," says Foskett. "Darian and I, to be fair mostly Darian, decided who would play what instrument on which song and then the three of us discussed who would sing which vocal part. It was decided that I would always sing the top harmony part even though Taylor Mills has the same top range as me. I thought it would sound more authentic with a male voice on the top part. Brian always sings the lead regardless of who ended up singing it on the actual recording. All in all, it is one unit of 11 people with one common goal: to make the music sound as great as it does coming out of your stereo! Brian's involvement with the vocal arrangements and lyrics were crucial to the live show. Whenever a question arose, he would answer very promptly and directly with the corrections. He knows everything about that record as if it were recorded last month."

The accompanying orchestras were organised by Paul Mertens, who wrote all of the charts. He followed Brian's original scheme when applicable and created parts to fortify different aspects of the show. Also employed for the second half of the summer 2000 tour was conductor Charles Floyd. A long time fan of Brian, he worked with Mertens to engage the orchestra to ensure each musician understood his parts. Foskett feels that Floyd brought a calming influence to the endeavour.

At this point, the orchestras would introduce the concerts with a new overture written by Van Dyke Parks. When the band arrived, Brian would sit centre stage behind an unused keyboard. This was a truly moving sight

*The concert some people said would never happen. Photo: Robert Mattau.*

for the diehard believers. Whilst The Beach Boys have continued touring, Brian's return to the stage has given fans a chance to see the man they most associate with the music that most profoundly affected their lives, *Pet Sounds*.

The concerts followed a broadly similar path. The first half mostly featured the adventurous songs that had led up to *Pet Sounds*, with "Kiss Me Baby", "Please Let Me Wonder", "'Til I Die" and "California Girls" sitting alongside a couple of newer items, "The First Time" and a tongue-in-cheek cover of The BareNaked Ladies' "Brian Wilson". After the intermission came the entirety of *Pet Sounds*, interrupted only by inter-song banter by Brian and some unnecessary audience applause during the songs. The encore unashamedly turned to the finest sing-alongs from the canon with "Good Vibrations", "Barbara Ann", "Surfin' USA" and "Fun Fun Fun", but ended, in a reflective hush, with "Love And Mercy".

"…Everyone in the sold-out crowd is wearing an I-can't-believe-this-is-really-happening look," *Mojo*'s critic enthused of the Chicago show. "These melodies belong with the best of Richard Rogers and George Gershwin… Their vocal harmonies are celestial, sung with a brio that would make Carl, Mike, Al, Bruce and Dennis proud… when Brian's voice cracks on some of the high notes, it puts many lumps in many throats."

For many fans, the Hollywood bowl gig represented the culmination of the tour.

"*Pet Sounds* changed my life for the better, and travelling to the Hollywood Bowl was a privilege and a pilgrimage," Andrew Loog Oldham

*Brian with his band, with Jeff Foskett on the right. Photo: Robert Mattau*

testifies. "For me it was like going to the Vatican and seeing the Pope."

"I went to the Santa Barbara Bowl, The Hollywood Bowl, and the final leg of the California tour at Humphreys On The Bay," says John Francis, one of many British fans who changed their holiday plans in 2000. "It was small and intimate, with loads of atmosphere from the lights on the yachts as the sun went down. But the Hollywood Bowl was the special one, the homecoming – everyone was there, including Marilyn and Tony Asher. God, it was great!"

Nancy Sinatra was also at the Hollywood Bowl. "Oooooh! The musicianship on that stage was superb," she enthuses.

According to Jeff Foskett, Brian was initially nervous but eventually learned to love being on the road. Foskett and Brian, who shared a bus with their wives, frequently rehearsed vocal parts with an acoustic guitar, and Jeff confirms that certain key CDs always came along: Gershwin's "Rhapsody In Blue," some Andy Williams, the main Spector hits and some Philly material for the occasional soul nights. Whilst still finding the demands of talking to people somewhat daunting, Brian is happy and relaxed when not 'on show.' He attends the majority of the band rehearsals and soundchecks, and if he is not there for any reason the band relies on what Darian Sahanaja calls the "integrity meters" for decision-making. Darian says that they get their reward in the best way musicians could, "There's nothing like seeing that smile on Brian's face when it all comes together…maybe even a proud smile." Foskett echoes this with, "Every morning I wake up and give thanks, I am so fortunate to have the best gig in the world."

American press reaction to the tour was glowing. *Rolling Stone* described a "heroic event" while *Time* recognised Brian's joy and observed that you would have to be "emotionally inert not to be happy for him in turn." *Press Enterprise* spoke of "the night's testaments to Brian's genius" and *The New York Times* heard "grand, fanciful, intricate songs". *The Los Angeles Times* called it a "long awaited and well deserved acknowledgement of Brian's position in pop music" whilst noting that "his legacy has never been fully and properly represented on stage by The Beach Boys". Old friends were similarly fulsome in their praise. Carol Kaye said simply that "His music is so wonderful, feeling alive in-person like it did when we cut his great tracks…it's eternal music". Film-maker Alan Boyd observed that "It has been too long for Brian to come out and share himself this way", whilst ex-promoter and long time friend Fred Vail was moved to write a special piece for the fan newsletter, *Breakaway*, after seeing the tour at Pine Knob,

"…It was just great to see Brian back on stage… I knew deep inside this was going to be a great event… Following the Pine Knob concert, Brian asked, 'Well, Fred, what did you think of the show?… Do you think it was a 10, Fred?' 'Yes, Brian, it was certainly a 10,' I answered. 'Wow!' said Bri, 'a 10 out of 10. That's really great!"

The *Breakaway* newsletter also featured ecstatic fan comments: "I have re-lived the concert a thousand times in my quieter moments", said one. "It was just incredible", enthused another, while others "were totally blown away at the concert last night". One fan evocatively saw watching the show as akin to "[having] completed some rite of passage and [having] been part of a spiritual experience all at the same time". Another fan, directing his praise towards the music's creator, said simply, "thank you for allowing us to share *Pet Sounds* with you."

"Brian [was] thrilled with the reactions," says Darian. "He looks to others for acceptance. That people have been so moved by the performances brings him true joy and keeps things in an upward motion."

Following the euphoria of the 2000 shows, people expected Brian to take things easier in 2001, but he has shown no sign of letting up. March 2001 saw the Brian Wilson Tribute Concert at the famed Radio City concert hall (see appendices), from which came the invitation for Brian to join some of Paul Simon's tour. After coming off the road from this tour, it is expected that he will work on a major new recording project with his touring band, though recent reports suggest that the eleven piece band may not stay together long enough for this to be possible.

A UK leg of the *Pet Sounds* tour was initially scheduled for July 2001, however the plans were put on back burner for a while. Britain's tax rules and a failure to secure sponsorship made the undertaking financially more challenging. However, as we go to press, three London dates have just been scheduled for January 2002. Given the album's tremendous history and stature here, Brian's thousands of fans are already eagerly awaiting the arrival of *Pet Sounds* live at what is arguably its spiritual home.

# EPILOGUE

*Pet Sounds* arose out of the mind of just one man, with help from talented friends and colleagues. It has already been shown that it has passed the test of time. Moreover, it has matured and revealed itself as a complex and layered piece of work still gaining appreciation by thousands of music fans around the world. My own relationship with it has been deepened during the writing of this book, and my initial fear that such close examination would lead to a diminution of enjoyment has proved groundless. Whether or not the album is the best pop/rock album of the twentieth century is impossible to truly say, as this is a question of subjectivity, but in the light of the strengths described in these pages one can make an incredibly strong case for it. What *can* be said loudly and clearly, is that this wonderful album is so well layered that it remains fascinating even through detailed inspection. *Pet Sounds* is so good that it attracts modern young listeners and musicians from every style.

That the album has had a long-reaching influence on many musicians is incontrovertible, not just in terms of covers of favourite songs, but a much more subtle, though quite wide, musical impact. More than anything, *Pet Sounds* created a precedent for a broad, intelligent and cohesive approach to album projects in terms of writing, recording and production. Only a few years before *Pet Sounds*, long players (as they had been called) were almost an industry add-on, subservient to the prime position of the mass-market single format. Phil Spector had been famously dismissive of the form and had concentrated almost exclusively on singles, to the extent that after the Righteous Brothers mega hit "You've Lost That Lovin' Feeling" he subbed out several of the album tracks to Bill Medley to produce. The standard long player form was two hits, their B-sides and seven or eight fillers. When *Pet Sounds* arrived, it fast became evident that its cohesiveness and quality had opened the doors to an entirely new pop rock form that was separate from the individual musical brilliance of the tracks. The Beatles were immediately driven to attempt to try and emulate it, and all around the industry musicians, writers and producers tried to adjust to a new way of thinking about recording. Brian Wilson had upped the ante. *Pet Sounds* was the new yardstick. Sections of the industry responded in different ways:

record companies saw long players in a new light and began to accept that their artists should be allowed to expand their ideas beyond the 45 rpm disc. Producers listened in awe to Brian's new sonorities, arrangers began to re-think percussive ideas and the breadth of instrumentation that was possible within pop. Groups began to realise that backing vocals were more than the simple unison that some had got away with, and writers realised that the pop world could cope with some deeper meanings than had often been the case. Brian Wilson was affecting everybody: some in little ways, others in major ways. Some musicians to this day worship at his altar, crafting note perfect re-creations of Beach Boys' sounds, or constructing tracks in ways that emanate directly from Brian's studio craft of the mid-sixties. For others, the effects are less tangible, but are there in the care and quality of the album form in which Brian was such a ground breaker, and indeed the use of the word "album" can be dated from the conceptual approach that he introduced. Music culture was built on a stronger and immensely richer base *after Pet Sounds*, and the listening audience's expectations were forever higher. Brian hadn't just made a wonderful album, he had revolutionised the whole industry.

Brian Wilson later referred to *Pet Sounds* as an "industrial success", meaning that it affected the way records were made. The care that he took with the writing, the arrangements, the rich instrumental sonorities and the note perfect harmonies have yet to be equalled, let alone bettered, by any comparable body of work. Echoes of his work can be found everywhere though, and have been evident for years from *Revolver* and *Pepper* onwards. The Carpenters, The Raspberries, Crosby, Stills and Nash, Eric Carmen, Curt Boettcher, Andrew Gold and more recently Eric Matthews, Jeff Foskett, Jeff Larson, and R.E.M. (especially "At My Most Beautiful" and parts of the recent *Reveal* album) are all Americans who owe an obvious debt to Brian in much of their work. In Britain, artists as varied as 10CC, Cliff Richard (with Tony Rivers' seventies input), Elton John, Chris Rainbow and the High Llamas all happily acknowledge debts, while cult London-based Frenchman Louis Philippe continues his wonderful Brian-influenced path. Add to this the countless fan and semi-professional recording and live Brian/Beach Boys inspired projects that have occurred on both sides of the Atlantic, around Europe and in Japan – almost without exception carried out with high production values and a whole lot of love – you are left with no doubt as to the richness of the legacy. Brian had created what David Leaf later called a "Wave Of Love", and that wave has just kept on rolling.

In the future, *Pet Sounds* will be recognised as a highlight of twentieth century music. Its influence has taken many forms, many of which are artistically subtle rather than mere imitation. Because the imaginative musicality of the album appeals so much to intelligent musicians, the influences are frequently ambiguous, and surface more clearly in production values. British writer/producer John Carter quickly realised, "After *Pet Sounds*, production became for me incredibly enjoyable as it seemed to have opened up endless possibilities of new combinations of instruments and sounds. It offered the chance of groundbreaking freedom of opportunity for what could be done within the confines of a pop production."

The extensive range of percussion effects is relatively easy to spot, and has been inspirational to younger musicians. Similarly, *Pet Sounds* encouraged popular music to employ unusual chord changes, key shifts, and the bass as a means to drive tracks or provide alternative motifs. It is as if Brian introduced a new range of colours to musician's palettes, and gave them the confidence to investigate new possibilities. However no artist has appeared able to use the wider palette with quite the same skill as Brian. Also, no artist has expanded the palette to such a degree – the only possible contender would be the Beatles album that *Pet Sounds* inspired.

"When *Sgt. Pepper* came out on CD, it awakened interest in that album to me," Paul McCartney told David Leaf in 1990. "I have a two-hour drive normally into London; I played *Sgt. Pepper* on the way in, and then *Pet Sounds* on the way out, and both of them more than held up...to me it's like 'What have people been doing in the meantime – where's the progress?'...I think they're very exciting, even though they're recorded quite primitively compared to now."

Modern advancements in music technology haven't necessarily been matched with advancements in inspiration. The "live" recording experience of a major project is far less likely today, and with that may have gone some of the spontaneity and creative invention that characterised Brian's work on *Pet Sounds*. He has said that constructing the album was largely a matter of trial and error within the studio. The final masterpiece surely arose from individual genius married to the experience and enthusiasm of caring musicians.

Today, there are many ways to listen to *Pet Sounds*. There is the original mono, the reconstructed stereo version that reveals extra details, the vocal tracks, the instrumental tracks, and the wealth of fascinating details available on the *Sessions* box set. Each has distinctive qualities. Brian has suggested more than once that the best way to listen to the whole album is through headphones in the dark. With the tremendous emotional content of the work, and the intricacies of the vocal and instrumental combinations, his advice is worth taking.

The album will continue to stand above the rest of The Beach Boys stellar canon of recordings, attracting future generations to the work of Brian Wilson. There can be little doubt that in 2066, 2166 and beyond, *Pet Sounds* will represent a towering pinnacle of popular culture.

David Leaf has described the album as "a spiritual love letter"; like the most benign chain letter, it has been spread its message around the globe.

It is, quite simply, Brian's gift to the world.

# Appendix 1
## THE PET SOUNDS RECORDING SESSIONS

The musicians who played at the *Pet Sounds* recordings were the cream of the L.A. players – veterans of thousands of sessions in the fifties and sixties. In many cases their own memories are dim and sometimes flawed, owing to the quantity of sessions they took part in and the fact that in many cases, including *Pet Sounds*, they would not have been aware of the title of the tracks they were working on. It is acknowledged that these details are unlikely to be 100% correct, and that mistakes and omissions could have occurred, but the following details are likely to be pretty close to the actual sessions that took place. Dates of the track recordings are difficult to totally pin down as various overdub sessions confuse the chronology, but what can be stated is that "Sloop John B" dates from July 1965, "Pet Sounds" (aka "Run James Run") from November 1965, and the original of "You Still Believe In Me" probably from September or October 1965. The rest of the track recordings took place during January, February and March 1966. Leaving aside Brian's lead or guide vocals, the bulk of the vocal sessions happened during March and April, with the exception of "Sloop John B," which was just before Christmas in late December 1965. Anomalies in dates given in other places suggest that any attempt to give definite dates would be likely to be erroneous.

**1 "Wouldn't It Be Nice" Gold Star/Engineer: Larry Levine
Capitol Master #55558-Take 21 is master.**

| | |
|---|---|
| Lead Vocal | Brian Wilson (verses), Mike Love (bridge) |
| Drums | Hal Blaine |
| Fender Bass | Carol Kaye |
| String bass | Lyle Ritz |
| Guitar | Jerry Cole, Barney Kessel, Bill Pitman, Ray Pohlman |
| Piano | Al de Lory |
| Tack piano | Larry Knechtel |

| | |
|---|---|
| Accordions | Carl Fortina, Frank Marocco |
| Timpani, bells | Frank Capp |
| Trumpet: | Roy Caton |
| Saxophones: | Steve Douglas, Plas Johnson, Jay Migliori |

### 2 "You Still Believe In Me" (AKA 'In My Childhood")
### Western/Engineer:
### Chuck Britz Capitol Master #55314-Take 23 is master.

| | |
|---|---|
| Lead vocal | Brian Wilson |
| | |
| Drums | Hal Blaine |
| Percussion | Jerry Williams |
| Bicycle bell, | |
| Finger cymbals | Julius Wechter |
| Fender Bass | Carol Kaye |
| String bass | Lyle Ritz |
| Guitars | Glen Campbell, Barney Kessel |
| Piano | Al De Lory |
| Trumpet | Roy Caton |
| Tenor Sax | Steve Douglas, Plas Johnson |
| Alto Sax | Bill Green, Jim Horn |
| Baritone Sax | Jay Migliori |

### 3 "That's Not Me" Western/Engineer: Chuck Britz Capitol Master #55591 – Take 15 is master.

| | |
|---|---|
| Lead vocal | Mike Love (verses), Brian Wilson & Mike Love (choruses) |
| | |
| Drums | Hal Blaine |
| Organ | Brian Wilson |
| Guitar | Carl Wilson |

(other players uncertain, but apparently do include Terry Melcher on tambourine)

### 4 "Don't Talk (Put Your Head On My Shoulder)" Engineer:
### H. Bowen David Capitol Master #55597 – Master take unknown

| | |
|---|---|
| Lead vocal | Brian Wilson |

| | |
|---|---|
| Drums | Hal Blaine |
| Percussion | Steve Douglas |
| Kettle drums | Frank Capp |
| Fender Bass | Carol Kaye |
| String Bass | Lyle Ritz |
| Guitars | Glen Campbell. Billy Strange |
| Organ | Al de Lory |
| Violins | Arnold Belnick, Ralph Schaeffer, Sid Sharp, |
| | Tibor Zelig |
| Cello | Joe Saxon |
| Viola | Norm Botnick |

## 5 "I'm Waiting For The Day" Engineer: H. Bowen David. Capitol Master #55865 – Take 14 is master.

| | |
|---|---|
| Lead vocal | Brian Wilson |
| | |
| Drums | Jim Gordon |
| Timpani, Bongos | Gary Coleman |
| Fender Bass | Carol Kaye |
| String Bass | Lyle Ritz |
| Guitar | Ray Pohlman |
| Piano | Al de Lory |
| Organ | Larry Knechtel |
| Flutes | Bill Green, Len Hartman, Jim Horn, |
| | Jay Migliori |

| | |
|---|---|
| Second session, string overdub | |
| Violins | Bill Kurasch, Lenny Malarsky, |
| | Ralph Schaeffer, Sid Sharp, |
| Cello | Justin DiTullio |
| Viola | Harry Hyams |

## 6 "Lets Go Away For Awhile" Western/Engineer Chuck Britz Capitol Master #55557 – Take 18 is master.

| | |
|---|---|
| Drums | Hal Blaine |
| Timpani, Vibes | Julius Wechter |
| Fender Bass | Carol Kaye |
| String Bass | Lyle Ritz |
| Guitars | Al Casey, Barney Kessel |

| | |
|---|---|
| Piano | Al de Lory |
| Trumpet | Roy Caton |
| Saxophones | Steve Douglas, Jim Horn, Plas Johnson, Jay Migliori |

Overdub:

| | |
|---|---|
| Flute | Jules Jacob |
| Violins | Jim Getzoff, Bill Kurasch, Lenny Malarsky, Jerry Reisler, Ralph Schaeffer, Sid Sharp, Tibor Zelig |
| Viola | Joe DiFiore, Harry Hyams |
| Cello | Justin DiTullio, Joe Saxon |

### 7 "Sloop John B" Western/Engineer: Chuck Britz. Capitol Master #53999 – Take 14 is master.

| | |
|---|---|
| Lead vocal | Brian Wilson & Mike Love |
| | |
| Drums | Hal Blaine |
| Percussion | Frank Capp |
| Fender Bass | Carol Kaye |
| String Bass | Lyle Ritz |
| Guitars | Al Casey, Jerry Cole, Billy Strange |
| Piano | Al de Lory |
| Flute | Steve Douglas |
| Saxophones | Jim Horn, Jay Migliori, Jack Nimitz |

Overdub on 29/12/65, 12-string guitar solo by Billy Strange and two lead vocals.

### 8 "God Only Knows" Western/Engineer:Chuck Britz. Capitol Master #55849 – Take 20 is master.

| | |
|---|---|
| Lead vocal | Carl Wilson |
| | |
| Drums | Hal Blaine |
| Percussion | Jim Gordon |
| Fender Bass | Carol Kaye |
| String Bass | Lyle Ritz |
| Guitars | Ray Pohlman |
| Pianos | Don Randi |
| Organ | Larry Knechtel |
| Accordions | Carl Fortina, Frank Marocco |

| | |
|---|---|
| French Horn | Alan Robinson |
| Saxophones | Bill Green, Len Hartman, Jim Horn, Jay Migliori |
| Violins | Lenny Malarsky, Sid Sharp |
| Viola | Darrel Terwilliger |
| Cello | Jesse Ehrlich |

(plus Mike Melvoin on harpsichord in all probability)

**9 "I Know There's An Answer" (AKA "Hang On To Your Ego")
Western/Engineer: Chuck Britz. Capitol Master #55596 – Take 12 is
master. (titled as on AFM contract, "Let Go Of Your Ego")**

| | |
|---|---|
| Lead Vocal | Mike Love & Alan Jardine (verses), Brian Wilson (choruses) |
| | |
| Drums | Hal Blaine |
| Tambourine | Julius Wechter |
| Fender Bass | Ray Pohlman |
| String Bass | Lyle Ritz |
| Guitars | Glen Campbell (probably banjo as well), Barney Kessel |
| Piano | Al de Lory |
| Organ | Larry Knechtel |
| Saxophones | Steve Douglas, Jim Horn, Jay Migliori |
| Bass Harmonica | Tommy Morgan |

**10 'Here Today" Sunset Sound/Engineer: Bruce Botnick
Capitol Master #55680 – Master take is constructed from take 11
and take 20 (from letter C out).**

| | |
|---|---|
| Lead vocal | Mike Love |
| | |
| Drums | Nick Martinis |
| Percussion | Frank Capp |
| Fender Bass | Ray Pohlman |
| String Bass | Lyle Ritz |
| Guitars | Al Casey, Mike Deasy |
| Piano | Don Randi |
| Organ | Larry Knechtel |
| Saxophones | Steve Douglas, Bill Green, Plas Johnson, |

|                      | Jay Migliori, Jack Nimitz |
|----------------------|---------------------------|
| Trombones            | Gail Martin, Ernie Tack   |

## 11 "I Just Wasn't Made For These Times" Gold Star/ Engineer: Larry Levine. Capitol Master#55598 – Take 6 is master.

| Lead vocal            | Brian Wilson                         |
|-----------------------|--------------------------------------|

| Drums, Temple Block   | Hal Blaine                           |
|-----------------------|--------------------------------------|
| Percussion            | Frank Capp                           |
| Fender Bass           | Ray Pohlma                           |
| String Bass           | Chuck Berghofer                      |
| Guitars               | Glen Campbell, Barney Kessel         |
| Piano                 | Don Randi                            |
| Harpsichord           | Mike Melvoin                         |
| Saxophone             | Steve Douglas, Plas Johnson, Jay Migliori |
| Harmonica             | Tommy Morgan                         |
| 'Theremin'            | Paul Tanner (see other appendix)     |

## 12 "Pet Sounds" (AKA "Run James Run") Western/Chuck Britz. Capitol Master #55848 – Take 3 is master.

| Drums        | Richie Frost                             |
|--------------|------------------------------------------|
| Fender Bass  | Carol Kaye                               |
| String Bass  | Lyle Ritz                                |
| Guitars      | Jerry Cole, Billy Strange, Tommy Tedesco |
| Saxophones   | Bill Green, Jim Horn, Plas Johnson, Jay Migliori |
| Trumpet      | Roy Caton                                |

## 13 "Caroline, No" Master #55536 – Take 17 is master.

Brian overdubbed second keyboard, second bass, drums in the vamp and saxophones.

| Vocal        | Brian Wilson                 |
|--------------|------------------------------|

| Drums        | Hal Blaine                   |
|--------------|------------------------------|
| Percussion   | Frank Capp                   |
| Fender Bass  | Carol Kaye                   |
| Guitars      | Glen Campbell, Barney Kessel |

| | |
|---|---|
| Ukulele | Lyle Ritz |
| Harpsichord | Al de Lory |
| Saxophones | Steve Douglas, Jim Horn, Plas Johnson, Jay Migliori |
| Flute/bass flute | Bill Green |

(plus Mike Melvoin on keyboard in all probability)

## 14 "Good Vibrations" Recorded at Gold Star 2/18/66
## (The session actually started at 11:30pm on 2/17/66)
## Take 28 is the master.

| | |
|---|---|
| Drums | Hal Blaine |
| Percussion | Frank Capp |
| Fender Bass | Ray Pohlman |
| String Bass | Lyle Ritz |
| Guitars | Al Casey, Billy Strange |
| Piano | Don Randi |
| Organ | Larry Knechtel |
| Saxophone | Steve Douglas, Bill Green, Plas Johnson, Jay Migliorl |
| 'Theremin' | Paul Tanner (see other appendix) |

## 15     "Trombone Dixie"

| | |
|---|---|
| Drums | Hal Blaine |
| Percussion | Jerry Williams |
| Latin Percussion/ Vibes | Julius Wechter |
| Fender Bass | Carol Kaye |
| String Bass | Lyle Ritz |
| Piano | Don Randi |
| Guitar | Jerry Cole, Barney Kessel, Billy Strange |
| Saxophone | Steve Douglas, Jay Migliori |
| Trombone | James Henderson, Lew McCreary |
| Trumpet | Roy Caton |

# Appendix 2
## THEREMINS AND OTHEREMINS

Amongst all the inventive sound blends that Brian Wilson constructed for *Pet Sounds*, perhaps the best known is his use of the 'theremin' on "I Just Wasn't Made For These Times" and on the later single "Good Vibrations." The problem is, as we have seen in the main text, that he wasn't actually using a true theremin, even though he thought that he was! The player Paul Tanner, who Brian had discovered at the session at Western with Barney Kessel was actually using a home made unit that worked on different principles to produce the variable oscillations.

A theremin is played by manipulating the magnetic waves around the unit in 3D space. The unit is never actually touched during the playing, and it is notoriously difficult to obtain precise and unwavering notes, which also points to the perfect notes on *Pet Sounds* emanating from another device. Paul's unit was based more on electric principles with a variable pitch oscillator, and he had developed it when he had observed just how difficult it was to get accurate notes from a true theremin. Realising how hard it was to play, he set about building a unit that produced a similar sound with more consistency and accuracy. His worked by running a pointer over a wire (thus varying the resistance) that had a pictorial approximation of keyboard positions beneath it. There was also an on/off contact switch to allow him to slide notes as well as producing individual ones. At the time apparently, Paul's unit was referred to as an electro-theremin even though it worked on quite different principles.

The true theremin was invented by the Russian Leon Theremin in 1918, and patented in 1928. Leon was quite a character by all accounts, spending time with Einstein, getting through three marriages without any divorces, and being both detained and set to work by the Russian government. He actually appeared at London's Alexandra Palace circa 1930 with his machine in concert.

Paul Tanner's oscillator box was also likely to have been the instrument responsible for the fifties TV show sounds on programmes like "My Favourite Martian" and "Lost In Space." It sought to achieve something similar to the Ondes-Martenot – invented by one Maurice Martenot in 1928 after its maker had met Leon Theremin some five years earlier. Whilst based upon Theremin's ideas, this had a five-octave keyboard that played only one note at a time, thus making chords impossible. The trademark glissandi effect was obtained by a ring pulled along a ribbon above the keyboard. This instrument was certainly used in the making of the Fireball XL5 and Captain Scarlet TV programmes, and has been written for by Messiaen and Honegger amongst others.

The instrument that Mike Love is observed playing in 60s film and TV clips is neither Paul's instrument nor an Ondes Martenot, but yet another entirely different instrument. This was a cross between a stylophone and an early synthesizer that appeared to be 'played' rather more like a steel guitar. It did not apparently produce anything like accurate theremin-like sounds.

True theremin sounds may variously be heard on recordings by The Bonzo Dog Doo Dah Band ("The Leg"), Lothar and The Hand People, Captain Beefheart and Led Zeppelin ("Whole Lotta Love"). Jimmy Page has subsequently been given a pocket theremin made by Long Wave Instruments of Britain.

For the "Pet Sounds" tour, Darian Sahanaja arranged to have a special unit constructed based on the original machine of Paul Tanner's that appeared on the record. Built by a Tanner protégé, Tom Polk, it has affectionately been dubbed the 'Tannerin' but as this has led to some confusions it is now being referred to as a 'slide theremin.' At a nineties Brian Wilson Tribute concert in London, a real Long Wave Instruments theremin was used and filmed for TV. It was played by Simon Beck, who managed to recreate the *Pet Sounds* notes very accurately whilst playing with Sean Macreavy's Landys group.

For further details of the original Paul Tanner machine, check out:
http://www.geocities.com/Vienna/1611/PTE-Tpage.html

For further details of the unit used on the tour, go to:
http://www.tompolk/Tannerin/Tannerin.html

For further details of the Ondes Martenot, go to:
http://www.audities.org/images/ondes_martenot_history.htm
or
http://www.obsolete.com/120_years/machines/martenot/

Anyone considering purchasing a real theremin (Pocket ones start around £100 and give great sounds that can be linked elsewhere) should contact:
Long Wave Instruments, 23 Ashley Lane, Hordle, Lymington, Hants,

SO41 0GB Phone 01425 610849 (Fax 01425 612838)
   Check them out at www.longwaveinstruments.com

And finally, as an intriguing additional note to the actual instrumentation used on the album, it has been suggested by a reliable source that the 'plucked/hit piano' notes on the introduction to "You Still Believe In Me" may actually have been re-dubbed using a marxophone. This is a little-known member of the autoharp family, which has sets of three strings placed together that are struck with hammers rather than strummed. However, repeated listening to the various *Pet Sounds* sessions and rehearsals CD issue suggest that this is not the case.

See a marxophone at http://www2.netdoor.com/~rlang/marxop.htm

# Appendix 3
## COVER VERSIONS AND INFLUENCED WORK
### Covers of *Pet Sounds* songs

Below is a selection of some of the more interesting covers that have been recorded over the years. Certain songs are more popular than others, and some have hardly been covered at all. Most of these will be long since deleted in their original forms, but may possibly be found on various CD compilations. (*) signifies an especially recommended recording. (M) signifies a song within a medley.

"Wouldn't It Be Nice" – Mike Post, Jeffrey Osborne, Bruce Johnston's symphonic Beach Boys, Cheeky Chaps, The Rubinoos.

"You Still Believe In Me" – Kirsty McColl (*), Beach Boys Family & Friends (sung by Carnie & Wendy), Anne Sofie von Otter, Gary Usher (symphonic).

"That's Not Me" – Huey Lewis & The News.

"Don't Talk (Put Your Head On My Shoulder)" – Linda Ronstadt (*), Birdwatchers, Vince Mendoza, David Garland, Hank Marvin, Ya Ya, Anne Sofie von Otter (*).

"I'm Waiting For The Day" – Peanut (aka Katie Kissoon)

"Let's Go Away For Awhile" – Sean Macreavy (with added vocals) (*), Brian Wilson Band (Roxy album 2000)

"Sloop John B" – Taste Of Honey, Collin Raye, Clydesiders, Barry McGuire, Welsh Rugby All Stars, The Spinners, Sunday Palladium Songsters.

"God Only Knows" – Taste Of Honey, Wild Honey, Tony Rivers and The Castaways, The Vogues, Diesel Park West, Mikiko Noda, Elvis Costello & the Brodsky Quartet, Captain and Tenille, Manhattan Transfer, Trygve Thue (M), Yellow Jackets, Judy Tzuke, Bruce Johnston's symphonic Beach Boys, PP Arnold, David Bowie, Glen Campbell, Neil Diamond, Justin Hayward, Monaco, Shadows, Teenage Fan Club, Portsmouth Sinfonia, New Edition, Nolans, State Of Mind, Jack Jones, Andy Williams, Gary Numan, Private Lives, Olivia Newton John, Joey Heatherington, London Symphony Orchestra, Sounds Orchestral, Portsmouth Sinfonia, Gary Usher (symphonic) plus many MOR artists.

"I Know There's An Answer" – Sonic Youth, Gary Gidman.

"Here Today" – Robb Storme Group, Bobby Vee, Mathilde Santing, The Reels, The Factotums, Lighting Seeds, 3D, MSG.

"I Just Wasn't Made For These Times" – Larry Carlton, Nick Waluska, David Garland.

"Pet Sounds" – Dos Dragsters, Brian Wilson Band (Roxy album 2000), Gary Usher (symphonic).

"Caroline No" – Nick De Caro, Dori Caymmi, Timothy B. Schmit, Sean Macreavy (*), Antony Thompson (*)**, Gary Usher (symphonic).

And for interest's sake:

"Hang On To Your Ego" – Frank Black [of The Pixies]

"Good Vibrations" – Hugo Montenegro, Little Joe Shaver and Devil Dog, Sea Cruise (M), Wild Honey, Todd Rundgren, The Troggs, Chris White, Sean Macreavy, Tony Rivers, Psychic TV, Chambers Brothers, The Kings Singers, California (M), Cathedral City Project (M), Frank Schobel, Shadows, J.D., Silver Blue, London Philharmonic Orchestra, Gary Usher (M) (symphonic).

** Brian apparently loves Anthony Thompson's version of "Caroline No" and keeps a copy near his bed. He went to see Anthony and his dad, Tony Rivers, playing in Los Angeles in Summer 2001.

The Beach Boys and Brian Wilson themselves have revisited some of the songs on various live and studio albums.

In many cases the above covers take the songs into fresh territory, far away from any 'Beach Boys' sound. New arrangements have included jazz, disco and instrumental interpretations, and a wide variety of other pop versions. It is certain that not all of them are worthy of hearing, but if I was to opt for just one it would certainly be the late, great Kirsty McColl's beautifully simple interpretation of "You Still Believe In Me." She must have made that recording with a lot of love in her heart, and her feeling for Brian's music was intensified by the simple message that was etched into the run out grooves of the original single – "God Bless Brian". She was a wonderful talent, and she will be sorely missed.

## Pet Sounds-influenced Work

The musical influences of *Pet Sounds* can be heard far beyond the covers listed above. The work of all these artists and the many others quoted in the main text contain echoes, moods, and feels that reflect Brian's work.

Aside from the obvious first step of appreciative musicians of the cover version option, the influences of *Pet Sounds* have taken many forms. Many of these are easy to spot, but many are deeper rooted and they emerge in a variety of ways – instrumental blends, percussion uses, vocal arrangements, melodic influences, lyrically emotionally, or simply the feel of the track. All the following are songs or albums that have stayed with me, and ones that can be recommended for seeking out by readers of this book.

**Singles:**

Nino Tempo – "Boys Town" (Tower, 1967)

Phil Spector's trusted sax player/student manages the perfect blend of Spector/*Pet Sounds* influences. Lyrically nodding to "God Only Knows", Tempo's gentle voice sits well on a track that subtly blends the best of both masters.

Sagittarius – "My World Fell Down" (Columbia, 1967)

Gary Usher produced this epic sound collage of shifting moods and vocals that brought Curt Boettcher into the camp to lead to further work under the California/California Music names.

Strawberry Children – "Love Years Coming" (Liberty, 1967)

Jim Webb masquerading under a suitably 'Summer Of love' name sings a lovely gentle song that ends on delightfully intertwined vocal harmonies that come straight from the feel of *Pet Sounds*.

The Garden Club – "Little Girl Lost And Found" (A&M, 1967)

Soft, sunshiny vocals on a song co-written and arranged by BW friend Tandyn Almer. The arrangements use instrumental combinations rooted in *Pet Sounds*, and it finishes with another gorgeous looping set of harmonies.

Dawn Chorus – "A Night To Be Remembered" (MCA, 1969)

An un-ashamed *Pet Sounds* inspired epic from Britain's John Carter (Ivy League, First Class et al) which lets influences seep into its every pore without any part being a blatant copy. See also much of Mr Carter's work with The Flowerpot Men.

Flash Cadillac & The Continental Kids – "Time Will Tell" (Private Stock, 1975)

A B-side that drew on many elements of The Beach Boys' '64-6 vocal and instrumental sounds, presented on a song and melody that Brian would have been proud of. Think very, very affectionate tribute.

Chris White – "Spanish Wine" (Charisma, 1976)

Melody and overall Wilsonian feel carry this fine song that actually was a British hit, and later covered by Lou Christie. A wistful looking-back on a past love that began an on-going love affair for Chris with Brian's music.

The Brian Bennett Band – "The Girls Back Home" (DJM, 1977)

The ex-Shadows purposefully sought out Tony Rivers to ensure a Brian Wilson feel on this great pop song. The several percussive elements, as might be expected, were strongly *Pet Sounds* influenced, and the vocal platform built on top was splendid.

Captain & Tennille – "I'm On My Way" (A&M, 1978)

For these two long-time Beach Boys associates, the influences were never so marked as on this *Pet Sounds*-styled percussion laden song which took them some way away from their MOR territory.


Route 28 – "Another Cape Cod Summer (This Year)" (Arf Arf 1983)

All Beach Boys summer harmonies on an good easy pop tune that builds to another slab of over-lapping fade-out harmonies that are obviously rooted in the *Pet Sounds* era.


Lindsay Buckingham – "D.W. Suite" (Mercury, 1984)

Lindsay brought many Wilson influences to Fleetwood Mac when he joined, but this solo B-side (A tribute to Dennis Wilson) utilises much of Brian's palate of juxtapositions, mood changes and walls of vocals.

R.E.M. – "At My Most Beautiful" (Warners 1999)

A beautiful song that effectively and expertly re-creates many *Pet Sounds* elements on a song that also catches the moods of the album. Pleasingly it was also a big hit.

**Specific Album Tracks:**

The Raspberries – "Overnight Sensation" and "Cruisin' Music" from album *Starting Over* (Capitol 1974)

Grandly written and executed by Eric Carmen for his group, these two tracks especially epitomise how The Raspberries could not really have existed without Brian Wilson's previous work.


Eric Carmen – "Someday" from album *Change Of Heart* (Arista, 1978)

Carmen's Brian influences continued into his solo career, and this song takes its mood and fine arrangement straight from the Wilson bag. Harmonies, bold percussion and time shifts are all here.


Chris Rainbow – "Dear Brian" from album *Looking Over My Shoulder*

(Polydor, 1978)

All Rainbow's album contain Wilson references, moods and song construction influences. This track, conceived as a letter to Brian, is a beautiful melodic wrap that was constantly championed by the late Roger Scott on London's Capitol Radio as one of the best Brian-inspired tracks.

The Dukes Of Stratosphear (XTC) – "Pale And Precious" from album *Psonic Psunspot* (Virgin, 1987)

The Dukes psychedelic pastiche album contained this lovely piece of Wilsonian delicacy to end the set. With quotes from both *Pet Sounds* and *Smiley Smile*, the track is a hidden little gem.

Andrew Gold (as The Fraternal Order Of The All) – "Love Tonight" and "Time Is Standing Still" from album *Greetings From Planet Love* (J-Bird, 1997)

With the album conceived as an affectionate pastiche of the sixties, The Beach Boys had to be in there. Gold chooses to perfectly evoke the *Pet Sounds* instrumental and vocal complexities on these two wonderful songs. As good an example of *PS* influences well used as you will find anywhere.

Jeffrey Foskett – "Everything I Need" from album *Twelve And Twelve* (New Surf, 2000)

Foskett enlists Brian's vocal help on this recent Wilson/Asher song, and inserts a lovely breakaway instrumental section into the song that draws totally of *Pet Sounds* sonorities and textures. Brian recorded it on his birthday and loved the track!

**Albums:**

Jan & Dean – *Save For A Rainy Day* album (J&D, 1967)

A completely thematic and 'mood' album that was planned and executed by Dean Torrence with the help of session players. It is impossible to conceive that this album would have happened without *Pet Sounds* as the trail blazer.

The 5th Dimension – *Magic Garden* album (Soul City, 1967)

This magnificent suite of songs was written by Jim Webb, drawing upon his love of Brian's music, with melodies, mood and vocal harmonies that suddenly emerged from the shrubbery. Also investigate Jim Webb solo albums.


Margo Guryan – *Take A Picture* album (Bell, 1968)

Inspired by hearing "God Only Knows" for the first time, Margo wrote and sung this gentle sixties 'buried treasure'. An experienced and knowledgeable musician, she drew upon Brian's bass lines in her song construction. The album has recently been re-released in the U.S. and Europe.


The Millennium – *Begin* album (Columbia, 1968)

Probably Curt Boettcher's finest hour, this intricately structured album arose from Curt's close attention to Brian's studio mastery. "Begin" features great contrasts, banks of vocals and instrumentation and lush production, and indicates at least one possible direction that Brian could have followed had he remained at the wheel.


Jeff Larson – *Watercolour Sky* album (New Surf, 1998)

Jeffrey Foskett's colleague's first album contains many gentle melodies and vocals that readily evoke the West Coast feel of Brian's best work. The California sound for the new century.


Louis Phillipe – *Azure* album (XIII Bis, 1998)

With obvious and subtle *Pet Sounds* mood influences on an album's worth of totally beautiful songs, this is a magnificent record. 100% recommended to anyone reading this book.


Linus Of Hollywood – *Your Favorite Record* album (Franklin Castle, 1999)

Current U.S. singer/songwriter discovers the treasure chest of Brian goodies, and uses them effectively and enthusiastically with strong vocal harmonies. Linus puts in a wealth of contrasting instrumentation.


Peter Lacey – *Beam* album (RP media, 2000)

Current British singer/songwriter offers an album of great songs heavily influenced by various stages of Brian's career. Peter's strength are in his melodies and lyrically imagery.


Splitsville – *Pet Soul* album (Houston Party, 2001)

Expanded from an original EP release, this new issue draws on two obvious 1965/6 influential albums, and includes songs called "Caroline Knows" and "The Love Songs of B. Douglas Wilson", and include mellotrons, accordians and banjos. Nuff said.


Sean Macreavy – *Through My Telescope* album (home production, 2001)

If *Pet Sounds* evoked a wistful melancholia, this thoroughly Wilson-influenced set of songs evokes a wonderful warmth with the full palate of colours. Sean was the musician who dared to put words to "Let's Go Away For Awhile" on his earlier *Dumb Angel* album. This one is like the rich sunset at the end of the film.

*Further influences with this Newcastle record shop.*

# Appendix 4
## THE PET SOUNDS SESSIONS BOX SET
### Capitol Records 7243 8 37662 2 2 (1996)

**Disc no. 1 THE STEREO MIX**

1 "Wouldn't It Be Nice"
*(B. Wilson/T. Asher/M. Love) Irving Music*

2 "You Still Believe In Me"
*(B.Wilson/T. Asher) Irving Music*

3 "That's Not Me"
*(B.Wilson/T. Asher) Irving Music*

4 "Don't Talk (Put Your Head On My Shoulder)"
*(Wilson/T. Asher) Irving Music*

5 "I'm Waiting For The Day"
*(B.Wilson/M. Love) Irving Music*

6 "Let's Go Away For Awhile"
*(Brian Wilson) Irving Music*

7 "Sloop John B"
*(Traditional; Arranged by B. Wilson) New Executive Music*

8 "God Only Knows"
*(B.Wilson/T. Asher) Irving Music*

9 "I Know There's An Answer"
*(B.Wilson/T. Sachen/M. Love) Irving Music*

10 "Here Today"
*(B.Wilson/T. Asher) Irving Music*

11 "I Just Wasn't Made For These Times"
   *(B.Wilson/T. Asher) Irving Music*

12 "Pet Sounds"
   *(Brian Wilson) Irving Music*

13 "Caroline, No"
   *(B.Wilson/T. Asher) Irving Music*

## SESSIONS – *PART 1*

14 "Sloop John B"    Highlights from tracking date
15 "Sloop John B"    Stereo backing track
16 "Trombone Dixie"    Highlights from tracking date
17 "Trombone Dixie"    Stereo backing track
18 "Pet Sounds"    Highlights from tracking date
19 "Pet Sounds"    Stereo track without guitar overdub
20 "Let's Go Away For Awhile"    Highlights from tracking date
21 "Let's Go Away For Awhile"    Stereo track without string overdub
22 "Wouldn't It Be Nice"    Highlights from tracking date
23 "Wouldn't It Be Nice"    Stereo backing track
24 "Wouldn't It Be Nice"    Stereo track with background vocals
25 "You Still Believe In Me"    Intro-Session
26 "You Still Believe In Me"    Intro-Master take
27 "You Still Believe In Me"    Highlights from tracking date
28 "You Still Believe In Me"    Stereo backing track

## Disc no. 2  SESSIONS – *PART 2*

1 "Caroline, No"    Highlights from tracking date
2 "Caroline, No"    Stereo backing track
3 "Hang On To Your Ego"    Highlights from tracking date
4 "Hang On To Your Ego"    Stereo backing track
5 "Don't Talk (Put Your Head On My Shoulder)"    Brian's instrumental demo
6 "Don't Talk (Put Your Head On My Shoulder)"    Stereo backing track
7 "Don't Talk (Put Your Head On My Shoulder)"    String overdub
8 "I Just Wasn't Made For These Times"    Highlights from tracking date

9  "I Just Wasn't Made For These Times"    Stereo backing track
10  "That's Not Me"    Highlights from tracking date
11  "That's Not Me"    Stereo backing track
12  "Good Vibrations"    Highlights from tracking date
13  "Good Vibrations"    Stereo backing track
14  "I'm Waiting For The Day"    Highlights from tracking date
15  "I'm Waiting For The Day"    Stereo backing track
16  "God Only Knows"    Highlights from tracking date
17  "God Only Knows"    Stereo backing track
18  "Here Today"    Highlights from tracking date
19  "Here Today"    Stereo backing track

## Disc no. 3 STACK-O-VOCALS

1  "Wouldn't It Be Nice"
2  "You Still Believe In Me"
3  "That's Not Me"
4  "Don't Talk (Put Your Head On My Shoulder)"
5  "I'm Waiting For The Day"
6  "Sloop John B"
7  "God Only Knows"
8  "I Know There's An Answer"
9  "Here Today"
10  "I Just Wasn't Made For These Times"
11  "Caroline, No"

## ALTERNATE VERSIONS

12  "Caroline, No" *Promotional Spot #1*
13  "Wouldn't It Be Nice"
14  "You Still Believe In Me"
15  "Don't Talk" *Vocal Snippet*
16  "I'm Waiting For The Day" *(Mike sings lead)*
17  "Sloop John B" *(Carl sings first verse)*
18  "God Only Knows" *(Sax Solo)*
19  "Hang On To Your Ego"
20  "Here Today"
21  "I Just Wasn't Made For These Times"
22  "Banana & Louie"

23  "Caroline, No" *(Original speed, stereo mix)*
24  Dog Barking Session *(Outtakes)*
25  "Caroline, No" *Promotional Spot #2*
26  "God Only Knows" *(with a capella tag)*
27  "Wouldn't It Be Nice"
28  "Sloop John B" *(Brian sings lead throughout)*
29  "God Only Knows" *(Brian sings lead)*
30  "Caroline, No" *(Original speed, mono mix)*

All tracks on Discs 1-3 Mixed January/February, 1996; except *on* Disc 3 (11-14, 16, 18, 19, 21, 25-27, 29, 30).

## BONUS DISC
The *Pet Sounds* album, the original mono mix, re-mastered in 1996

1   "Wouldn't It Be Nice"
2   "You Still Believe In Me"
3   "That's Not Me"
4   "Don't Talk (Put Your Head On My Shoulder)"
5   "I'm Waiting For The Day"
6   "Let's Go Away For Awhile"
7   "Sloop John B"
8   "God Only Knows"
9   "I Know There's An Answer"
10  "Here Today"
11  "I Just Wasn't Made For These Times"
12  "Pet Sounds"
13  "Caroline, No"

*All* Songs Irving Music, Inc. BMI
Except "Sloop John B" and "Trombone Dixie", New Executive Music

Special note: There are also some hidden 'snippets' tracks to find.

## Statement of Purpose

In the preparation of the mono *Pet Sounds* CD bonus disc, every effort has been made to make this historic album sound the way it did in the studio when Brian Wilson produced it in 1966. The original tape was transferred using a special custom 24 bit analog converter, and all equalization was performed in the analog domain in order to better preserve the sound of the recordings. No re-mixing was attempted as it was felt that the result would not be true to Brian's vision of the album. This CD has been digitally re-mastered using the l-IDCD system which offers a dramatic improvement over conventional 16 bit mastering systems.

Mark Linett
May, 1996

# Appendix 5
## *PET SOUNDS* CHART HISTORY

**U.S. Album Charts (*Billboard*)**

Entered May 28th 1966, and went – 106 – 49 – 25 – 14 – 11 – 10 – 11 – 13 – 14 – 14 – 13 – 16 – 19 – 20 – 20 – 34 – 32 – 28 – 27 – 28 – 32 – 38 – 40 – 44 – 53 – 69 – 71 – 89 – 88 – 104 – 109 – 113 – 113 – 115 – 122 – 119 – 116 – 115 – 110 – off Feb 25$^{th}$ 1967

With "Carl And The Passions" as additional album, from June 3rd 1972 – 200 – 102 – 79 – 64 – 62 – 53 – 50 – 50 – 56 – 58 – 58 – 62 – 64 – 66 – 91 – 91 – 105 – 118 – 139 – 160 – off Oct 21$^{st}$ 1972

**U.S. Singles Charts (*Billboard*)**

"Sloop John B" entered 26th March 1966 – 112 – 68 – 35 – 13 – 8 – 4 – 3 – 5 – 9 – 15 – 27 – 33 – off 18th June 1966

"Wouldn't It Be Nice" entered 30th July 1966 – 84 – 62 – 51 – 26 – 16 – 11 – 11 – 8 – 9 – 23 – 45 – off 15th October 1966

"God Only Knows" entered 6th August 1966 – 109 – 81 – 64 – 51 – 45 – 42 – 40 – 39 – 45 – off 1st October 1966

**U.K. Albums Chart (*NME* – top ten only printed until 17th December 1966, thereafter top 15)**

"Pet Sounds" entered 9th July 1966 – 6 – 3 – 3 – 2 – 2 – 3 – 3 – 3 – 3 – 3 – 4 – 4 – 4 – 4 – 4 – 5 – 5 – 5 – 7 – 7 – 9 – 9 – 9 – off 17th December 1966, re-entered new top 15 chart on 14th January 1967 – 13 – 15 – off 28th January 1967

**U.K. Singles Chart (*NME* top 30)**

"Sloop John B" entered 23rd April 1966 – 19 – 11 – 5 – 3 – 2 – 5 – 7 – 9 – 13 – 16 – 20 – 29 – 26 – off 23rd July 1966

"God Only Knows" entered 30th July 1966 – 19 – 13 – 7 – 3 – 2 – 2 – 3 – 5 – 10 – 19 – off 8th October 1966

# Appendix 6
# BIBLIOGRAPHY

The following books, booklets, magazines and articles were consulted or recalled during the writing of this book. The author acknowledges the quality and excellent research contained within the writings.

*The Beach Boys and The California Myth* by David Leaf. Grosset And Dunlap, New York 1979. 2nd Edition Courage Books, 1985.

*The Beach Boys* by Byron Press. Ballantine New York, 1979.

*Heroes And Villains* by Stephen Gaines. Macmillan, 1986.

*Wouldn't It Be Nice* by Brian Wilson and Todd Gold. Harper Collins, 1991.

*The Nearest Faraway Place: Brian Wilson, The Beach Boys and the Southern California Experience* by Timothy White. Henry Holt, 1994.

*Surf's Up: The Beach Boys On Record 1961-1981*. Pierian Press, 1982.

*Our Favourite Recording Sessions* by Stephen J. McParland. CMusic Books, 2000.

*Smile, Sun, Sand & Pet Sounds* compiled by Stephen J McParland. CMusic Books 1999.

*The California Sound: The Musical Biography Of Gary Usher*, Volume 1 By Stephen J. McParland. CMusic Books 2000.

*Hal Blaine and The Wrecking Crew* by Hal Blaine with David Goggin. MixBooks, 1990.

*Look! Listen! Vibrate! Smile!* compiled by Dominic Priore. Last Gasp, 1995.

*Back To The Beach. A Brian Wilson & The Beach Boys Reader* edited by Kingsley Abbott. Helter Skelter, 1997.

*Add Some Music To Your Day* edited by Don Cunningham and Jeff Bleiel. Tiny Ripple, 2000.

*The Beach Boys – In Their Own Words* by Nick Wise. Omnibus, 1994.

*Brian Wilson & The Beach Boys: How Deep Is The Ocean?* by Paul Williams. Omnibus, 1997.

*The Beach Boys* by Andrew Doe and John Tobler. Omnibus, 1997.

*Booklet for The Beach Boys CD Box Set* by David Leaf, Mark Linett and Andy Paley. Capitol Records, 1993.

*Booklet for The Pet Sounds Sessions Box Set* by David Leaf and Mark Linett. Capitol Records, 1996.

*Booklet of The Making Of Pet Sounds* by David Leaf. Capitol Records, 1996.

Various sleeve notes from the Beach Boys Capitol Twofers CDs by David Leaf. Capitol Records, 1990.

Various copies of *Breakaway with Brian Wilson* edited by Brian Battles, *Beach Boys Australia* magazine edited by Stephen J. McParland, and *Endless Summer Quarterly* edited by Lee Dempsey and David Beard.

Various copies of *Record Collector* magazine. Parker Mead.

Various copies of *Goldmine* magazine.

*Performing Songwriter* Vol 3 Issue 18, May/June 1996.

*40 Years Of NME Charts.* Boxtree, 1992.

*30 Years Of NME Album Charts.* Boxtree, 1993.

# Appendix 7
## ACROSS THE GENERATIONS

By way of underscoring the extent to which I believe that the album appeals across the generations, I am very happy to include my own nineteen-year-old son's thoughts…

*"There are few things that remain constant whilst you grow up, but for long as I can remember I've had the sound of the Beach Boys engraved onto my eardrums. I can't remember ever having heard any of their songs for the first time. Endless hours of CDs in the background and tapes being played in the car ensured that, by the time I had developed an appreciation for music, I accidentally knew pretty well every Beach Boys song up until* Holland *(including the half formed songs of* Smile*). I'm quite sure that my father would refer to this as 'education.'*

*"As my tastes in music began to mature, I started to work my way through the vast expanse of my dad's record collection. I found some of the most exciting and inspired albums ever made: Love's* Forever Changes, *The Band's second album, Big Star's* #1 Record. *I also got into Fairport Convention, The Byrds, The Millennium, Jefferson Airplane and many more wonderful bands that sound as fresh today as I can only imagine they would have done 35 years ago.*

*"It was while I was hearing all these bands for the first time that I decided to sit down and really listen to* Pet Sounds. *Despite knowing all the individual tracks, I had never put them in the context of the album. This gave the music a whole new light for me, and I started to see what a masterpiece it was. It's not just the sublimely beautiful songs, or the lovingly constructed harmonies that struck me as genius, it was the incredible sound created from Brian's almost bizarre, eclectic use of instruments.*

*"*Pet Sounds *was more than just the sound of a band playing, it was an entire orchestra tailor made by Brian to perfectly complement the songs. It broke out of a musical shell and ventured into new territory, but still maintained the type of melody and construction that can take most people a lifetime to perfect. This is the reason I love* Pet Sounds *so much: it blows*

*your mind and touches your heart at the same time. The music is absolutely timeless, and it's the type of record that could only happen once. It will last forever.*

– Luke Abbott

This event was in the planning for many months, and was designed to show America and the world just how respected Brian and his music was by his fellow musicians. After various star renditions of a variety of Beach Boys hits (Including "California Girls"/"Help Me Rhonda" – Ricky Martin, a wonderfully different acoustic "Surfer Girl" – Paul Simon, "In My Room" – David Crosby/Carly Simon/Jimmy Webb, "Don't Worry Baby" – Billy Joel, "Good Vibrations" – Ann & Nancy Wilson of Heart, "Surf's Up" – Vince Gill/David Crosby/Jimmy Webb and "You're So Good To Me" – Wilson Phillips), Brian took the stage and surprised everyone with a powerful version of "Heroes And Villains" followed by "Lay Down Burden" with Carl's son Justyn Wilson on guitar.

The second half of the concert gave the 6,000-strong crowd a real treat as it was to be an all-star rendition of *Pet Sounds*. Elton John joined Brian for "Wouldn't It Be Nice", which was followed by a poignant version of "You Still Believe In Me" from Brian's daughters Carnie and Wendy. Jubilant Sykes led on "That's Not Me", whilst Ann and Nancy Wilson sang "Don't Talk (Put Your Head On My Shoulder)". Matthew Sweet, who had sung "Sail On Sailor" with Darius Rucker earlier, provided "I'm Waiting For The Day" before Brian's band gave their usual perfect take on "Let's Go Away For Awhile". David Crosby handled "Sloop John B" in folky vein, and Elton John provided a strong version of "God Only Knows". "I Know There's An Answer" came from Darius Rucker, and Jimmy Webb returned to deliver "Here Today". Aimee Mann and Michael Penn led on "I Wasn't Made For These Times", leading into the second band instrumental "Pet Sounds".

It could really only be Brian himself singing the album's closer "Caroline No", and he duly performed a stunning version. The rousing encore saw Brian strapping on his bass with the company returning to the predictable singalongs of "Barbara Ann", "Surfin' USA" and "Fun, Fun, Fun", which it undoubtedly was for all concerned. Brian closed the show with a simple "Love And Mercy", a song that has taken on increasing significance in the Wilson canon over the last few years, and even more so since the tragedy of

11$^{th}$ September, 2001. The show was filmed for the TNT channel, and an edited edition was broadcast on 4th July 2001 in the U.S.

"It was truly a scene from Dante backstage," Jimmy Webb reflected on this special show, in an email a few days after. "Twenty-one performers who were being hustled around like pawns on a chessboard. To give you an idea: there were six rock and roll hall of famers, two knights of the realm, another baker's dozen of songwriters hall of famers and five hundred other people working in the building including Vince and Amy Gill's two and a half-week old daughter Corina who lay patiently on her mother's lap and made not a peep through the whole show. It was really quite something. I didn't shed a tear until Brian dedicated a song to 'my brothers Carl and Dennis...they died.' and then I just lost it. Just like I'm losing it right now."

"There was a wonderful feeling of belonging to a special group of people backstage," Webb continued, in a more recent mailing. "Perhaps, knowing entertainers the way I do, it was a resolution in some way for many of us. The secret nightmare of not being asked to join the club was officially over. Many people there were almost – shall I say – desperate to communicate to someone, anyone, everyone, *Brian* in particular, the impact of his music on their own personal cosmos. To have had a body of work be so influential in one's own musical development and then to look about at such a vast reservoir of similarly induced inspiration among the other artists, all admired, all admiring, was almost eerie. Spooky too, that we were listening and participating in a live performance of the album called *Pet Sounds* because it had become just that. Our favourites, our pet sounds."

# A POEM FROM STEPHEN J. KALINICH...

Steve Kalinich is a poet and lyricist living in Los Angeles, and is the only credited person to have written with all three Wilson brothers. He remains friends with Brian, his daughters and ex-wife Marilyn. After attending the *Pet Sounds* concert, he was moved to write this poem especially for this book.

LOVE

BRIAN WILSON NEW YEARS EVE
2000

ENTERING THE NEW MILLENIUM
WITH
PET SOUNDS

BRIAN WILSON
WHO HAS TOUCHED THE PLANET
WITH SUCH BEAUTIFUL,
FUN,
EXCITING MUSIC
SO MUCH OF IT.
HAS PERHAPS HIT HIS ZENITH
WITH PET SOUNDS.
A DAZZLING
POETIC
SYMPHONIC MASTERPIECE.


THE LOVE JUST POURS OUT
EACH NOTE.
IT IS A TAPESTRY

OF SOUNDS AND FEELINGS
WOVEN TOGETHER
LIKE FINE SILK
WITH A DASH OF BEETHOVEN.
HIS PRESENCE IS MAGNIFICENT.
HIS OVERCOMING THE OBSTACLES
THE SHYNESS
HIS STRUGGLES
HIS COMING TO LIFE!
THIS SHOW WAS SO MUCH MORE POWERFUL
THAN THE LAST ONE I WENT TO.
I WENT TWICE.
ONCE TO SANTA BARBARA
AND TO HOLLYWOOD BOWL.
I GOT SUCH A CHARGE
OUT OF SEEING HIM MOVE
WITH THE MIKE IN HIS HAND.
THERE I WAS
SITTING WITH
MARILYN,
DANIEL
AND P.F. SLOAN.
IT WAS SO GOOD SPIRITED AND HEARTED.
IT WAS HONEST
SINCERE
GENUINE.
YOU FELT HIS PAINS
HIS STEP BY STEP
RISING ABOVE THEM
BRINGING THESE BEAUTIFUL SONGS
TO THE WORLD.
IT WAS REAL.
WHAT A WAY
TO BRING IN THE MILLENNIUM.
IT IS AN HONOR
TO HAVE WORKED WITH HIM
TO ONCE AGAIN
EXPERIENCE HIS AUTHENTICITY.
THERE WAS A SWEET MERCY
TO THE EVENING
A REBIRTH

FOR ME ANYWAY.
HIS SONGS
OPEN UP THE GOOD
AND FUN WITHIN US-
TOUCH AND
HEAL OUR WOUNDS-
SHARE OUR SORROWS
OUR HOPES
OUR LOVES.
"DON'T WORRY BABY"
"IN MY ROOM"
"GOD ONLY KNOWS"
"CAROLINA NO".
ALL THE SONGS!
WHAT A WAY TO BEGIN THIS NEXT CENTURY.
IT IS WONDERFUL
THAT THIS BEING
CONTINUES TO GIVE THESE GIFTS
OF SONGS TO US
FROM HIMSELF.
I LOVE IT! I LOVE IT!
TO SEE SO MANY FRIENDS
AND PEOPLE
I DO NOT EVEN KNOW
HAVING SUCH A GREAT TIME.
THE PLAYERS
WERE FABULOUS-
IT LIFTED ME INTO A NEW CENTURY.
IT COULD NOT HAVE BEEN
MORE PRESENT
MORE BEAUTIFUL-
GOD WHAT A SHOW.

*Photo: Robert Mattau.*

# Other Titles available from Helter Skelter.

## Coming Soon from Helter Skelter:

## Early 2002

### Ashley Hutchings: The Guvnor and the Rise of Folk Rock – Fairport Convention, Steeleye Span and the Albion Band
By Geoff Wall and Brian Hinton £12.99
As founder of Fairport Convention and Steeleye Span, Ashley Hutchings is the pivotal figure in the history of folk rock. This book draws on hundreds of hours of interviews with Hutchins and other folk-rock artists and paints a vivid picture of the scene that also produced Sandy Denny, Richard Thompson, Nick Drake, John Martyn and Al Stewart.

### Gram Parsons: God's Own Singer
By Jason Walker £12.99
Brand new biography of the man who pushed The Byrds into country-rock territory on Sweethearts of The Rodeo, and then quit to form the acclaimed Flying Burrito Brothers. Parsons' second solo record, Grievous Angel, is a haunting masterpiece of country soul. By the time the album was released, Parsons had been dead for 4 months. He was 26 years old.

## Summer 2001

## Currently Available

### Calling Out Around the World: A Motown Reader
Edited by Kingsley Abbott £13.99
With a foreword by Martha Reeves, this is a unique collection of articles which tell the story of the rise of a black company in a white industry, and its talented stable of artists, musicians, writers and producers. Included are rare interviews with key figures such as Berry Gordy, Marvin Gaye, Smokey Robinson and Florence Ballard as well as reference sources for collectors and several specially commissioned pieces.

### Razor Edge: Bob Dylan and The Never-ending Tour
Andrew Muir £12.99
Respected Dylan expert Andrew Muir documents the ups and downs of this unprecedented trek, and finds time to tell the story of his own curious meeting with Dylan.
   Muir also tries to get to grips with what exactly it all means – both for Dylan and for the Bobcats: dedicated Dylan followers, like himself, who trade tapes of every show and regularly cross the globe to catch up with the latest leg of The Never Ending Tour.

### The Return of The Last Gang in Town: The Story and Myth of the Clash
By Marcus Gray £14.99
Revised, updated and completely overhauled, mammoth history of the greatest rock 'n' roll band of the modern rock era, that is also a detailed and erudite history of punk and the punk fall out years.
"If you're a music fan … it's important you read this book." *Record Collector*
"A valuable document for anyone interested in the punk era." *Billboard*

### King Crimson: In The Court of King Crimson
By Sid Smith £14.99
King Crimson's 1969 masterpiece In The Court Of The Crimson King, was a huge U.S. chart hit. The band followed it with 40 further albums of consistently challenging, distinctive and innovative music. Drawing on hours of new interviews, and encouraged by Crimson supremo Robert Fripp, the author traces the band's turbulent history year by year, track by track.

### I've Been Everywhere: A Johnny Cash Chronicle
By Peter Lewry £12.99
A complete chronological illustrated diary of Johnny Cash's concerts, TV appearances, record releases, recording sessions and other milestones. From his early days with Sam Phillips in Memphis to international stardom, the wilderness years of the mid-sixties, and on to his legendary prison concerts and his recent creative resurgence with the hugely successful 2000 release, *American Recording III: Solitary Man.*

### Sandy Denny: No More Sad Refrains
By Clinton Heylin £13.99
Paperback edition of the highly acclaimed biography of the greatest female singer-songwriter this country has ever produced.

### Emerson Lake and Palmer: The Show That Never Ends
George Forrester, Martin Hanson and Frank Askew £14.00
Prog-rock supergroup Emerson Lake and Palmer, were one the most successful acts of the seventies and, in terms of sound, artistic vision and concept, operated on a scale far in excess of any rivals.
   Drawing on years of research, the authors have produced a gripping and fascinating document of one of the great rock bands of the seventies.

### Animal Tracks: The Story of The Animals
Sean Egan £12.99
Sean Egan, author of the acclaimed Verve biography, *Starsailor* (Omnibus, 1998) has enjoyed full access to surviving Animals and associates and has produced a compelling portrait of a truly distinctive band of survivors.

### Like a Bullet of Light: The Films of Bob Dylan
CP Lee £12.99
In studying in-depth an often overlooked part of Dylan's oeuvre, *Like A Bullet of Light* forms a compelling portrait of an enigmatic artist as keen to challenge perceptions in the visual medium as in his better known career in music.

### Rock's Wild Things: The Troggs Files
Alan Clayson and Jacqueline Ryan £12.99
Respected rock writer Alan Clayson has had full access to the band and traces their history from 60s Andover rock roots to 90s covers, collaborations and corn circles. The Troggs Files also features the first ever publication of the full transcript of the legendary "Troggs Tapes," said to have inspired the movie *This is Spinal Tap*, together with an exhaustive discography and many rare photos

### Waiting for the Man: The Story of Drugs and Popular Music
by Harry Shapiro UK Price £12.99
Fully revised edition of the classic story of two intertwining billion dollar industries. "Wise and witty." *The Guardian*

### The Sharper Word: A Mod Reader
Edited by Paolo Hewitt (available November 1999) UK price:£12.99
Hugely readable collection of articles documenting one of the most misunderstood cultural movements

### Dylan's Daemon Lover: The Tangled Tale of a 450-Year Old Pop Ballad
by Clinton Heylin UK price £12.00
Written as a detective story, Heylin unearths the mystery of why Dylan knew enough to return "The House Carpenter" to its 16th century source.

### Get Back: The Beatles' *Let It Be* Disaster
by Doug Sulpy & Ray Schweighardt UK price £12.99
No-holds barred account of the power struggles, the bickering, and the bitterness that led to the break-up of the greatest band in the history of rock 'n' roll. "One of the most poignant Beatles books ever." *Mojo*

### XTC: Song Stories – The Exclusive & Authorised Story
by XTC and Neville Farmer UK Price £12.99
"A cheerful celebration of the minutiae surrounding XTC's music with the band's musical passion intact … high in setting-the-record-straight anecdotes. Superbright, funny, commanding." *Mojo*

### Like The Night: Bob Dylan and the Road to the Manchester Free Trade Hall
by CP Lee UK Price £12.00
In 1966 at the height of Dylan's protest-singing popularity he plugged in an electric guitar to the outrage of folk fans who booed and jeered. Finally, in Manchester, fans branded him Judas. "Essential Reading" *Uncut*

### Born in the USA: Bruce Springsteen and the American Tradition
by Jim Cullen UK Price £9.99
"Cullen has written an excellent treatise expressing exactly how and why Springsteen translated his uneducated hicktown American-ness into music and stories that touched hearts and souls around the world." *Q****

### Back to the Beach: A Brian Wilson and the Beach Boys Reader
Ed Kingsley Abbott UK Price £12.99
"A detailed study and comprehensive overview of the BBs' lives and music, even including a foreword from Wilson himself by way of validation. Most impressively, Abbott manages to appeal to both die-hard fans and rather less obsessive newcomers." *Time Out* "Rivetting!" **** *Q* "An essential purchase." *Mojo*

### A Journey Through America with the Rolling Stones
by Robert Greenfield UK Price £9.99
Featuring a new foreword by Ian Rankin
   This is the definitive account of their legendary '72 tour.
   "Filled with finely-rendered detail … a fascinating tale of times we shall never see again" *Mojo*

### Bob Dylan
by Anthony Scaduto UK Price £10.99
The first and best biography of Dylan. "The best book ever written on Dylan" *Record Collector* "Now in a welcome reprint it's a real treat to read the still-classic Bobography". *Q*****

## Mail Order

All Helter Skelter, Firefly and SAF titles are available by mail order from the world famous Helter Skelter bookshop.

You can either phone or fax your order to Helter Skelter on the following numbers:

Telephone: +44 (0)20 7836 1151 or Fax: +44 (0)20 7240 9880
Office hours: Mon-Fri 10:00am – 7:00pm,
Sat: 10:00am – 6:00pm, Sun: closed.

Postage prices per book worldwide are as follows:

| | |
|---|---|
| UK & Channel Islands | £1.50 |
| Europe & Eire (air) | £2.95 |
| USA, Canada (air) | £7.50 |
| Australasia, Far East (air) | £9.00 |
| Overseas (surface) | £2.50 |

You can also write enclosing a cheque, International Money Order, or registered cash. Please include postage. DO NOT send cash. DO NOT send foreign currency, or cheques drawn on an overseas bank. Send to:

Helter Skelter Bookshop,
4 Denmark Street, London, WC2H 8LL, United Kingdom.
If you are in London come and visit us, and browse the titles in person!!

Email: helter@skelter.demon.co.uk
Website: http://www.skelter.demon.co.uk